John Jenkins

The Laws relating to religious Liberty and Public Worship

John Jenkins

The Laws relating to religious Liberty and Public Worship

ISBN/EAN: 9783743329157

Manufactured in Europe, USA, Canada, Australia, Japa

Cover: Foto ©ninafisch / pixelio.de

Manufactured and distributed by brebook publishing software (www.brebook.com)

John Jenkins

The Laws relating to religious Liberty and Public Worship

TABLE OF CONTENTS.

CHAPTER I.

THE RISE AND PROGRESS OF RELIGIOUS LIBERTY IN ENGLAND.

	PAGES.
Religious Condition of Europe in the Middle Ages	3–4
Entirely Subject to the Papal Dominion	5–6
Appearance of Martin Luther in the beginning of the Sixteenth Century	7
His Character	8
His Opposition to the Papal Power	9–11
His Zeal, Determination, and Successful Career	13
The Reformation	14
Effects of the Reformation in England	15–16
Rise of the Puritans	16–18
Edward the Sixth	18
His Reign favourable to the Puritans	ib.
His Promising Character	ib.
His Short Reign and Early Death	ib.
Succeeded by his sister Mary	ib.
The Queen a Romanist	19
Her attempts to re-establish Romanism	ib.
Her Persecution of the Protestant Reformers	20

Revived the Penal Laws enacted in the reigns of the earlier Monarchs against the Lollards or Protestants	20
Established the Court of Ecclesiastical Commission	ib.
Presided over first by Bishop Gardiner, the Chancellor	ib.
Afterwards by Bishop Bonner	ib.
Arbitrary proceedings of this Court	ib.
Equal in effect to the Inquisition in Spain . .	ib.
Martyrdom of Bishops Hooper, Latimer, and Ridley	ib.
Sanguinary Character of this Reign	ib.
Character of Mary, her short Reign, and comparatively early Death	21
Elizabeth succeeded to the Throne	ib.
Joy of the Protestants at her Accession . . .	ib.
High Church and despotic Character of Elizabeth .	22
Caused to be passed the Act of Ecclesiastical Supremacy	ib.
Provisions of this Act	ib.
The Queen established the High Commission Court	23
Arbitrary Character and Proceedings of this Court .	ib.
Persecution of the Puritans	24
Their Increase	25
Their wider departure from the Established Church	27
Appearance of Robert Brown	28
His Doctrines and Ministry	ib.
Suffered much Persecution	29
Removed to Middleburgh, in Holland . . .	ib.
Indifferent Character of Brown	ib.
Appearance of Barrow and Ainsworth . . .	30
Their consistent Character	ib.
Steady Progress of Puritanism notwithstanding much Persecution	ib.

CONTENTS.

	PAGES.
Death of Grindall, Archbishop of Canterbury	32
Succeeded by Whitgift	ib.
His Enmity to the Puritans	ib.
His Servility to the Queen	ib.
Court of Ecclesiastical Commission reconstructed with additional powers	33
Mr. Hume's Testimony of its Character	ib.
Its Severity to the Puritans	34
Martyrdom of Barrow, Greenwood, and Penry	35
Passing of the Act to Retain her Majesty's Subjects in due obedience	ib.
Its severe Provisions	ib.
Designed to suppress Puritanism	36
Appearance of John Robinson	37
Regarded as Founder of the Independents	ib.
Removed with a portion of his Church to Leyden, in Holland	ib.
Congregationalism not adapted to the character of the Dutch People	ib.
It languished in Holland	ib.
Removal of a portion of the Church in Leyden to New England in 1620	38
Followed by the remainder of the Church after the death of Robinson in 1624	ib.
Good Fortune of America by the emigration thither of the "Pilgrim Fathers"	39
They founded its greatness	ib.
Summary of the Religious Character of Elizabeth's reign	ib.
Its systematic Persecution of the Puritans	40
Steady Increase of Nonconformity	41
Death of Elizabeth	ib.
Succeeded by James, King of Scotland	42

CONTENTS.

	PAGES.
Joy of the Nonconformists at his Accession	42
Expressed by their Petition, called "Millenary"	ib.
Their subsequent Disappointment	43
Vacillation and Deceit of the King	ib.
His Hostility to the Puritans	ib.
The King summoned a Conference between the High Church and Puritan parties, held at Hampton Court	ib.
The vain King presided over the Conference	ib.
Subjects of Discussion	44
Unsuccessful Result of the Conference	ib.
The Liturgy was amended	ib.
The Bible was translated into the present Authorised Version	ib.
The King's persecuting Disposition	45
Restrained by the public opinion of his Subjects	ib.
Bancroft was Archbishop of Canterbury	46
His Hostility to the Puritans	ib.
Was Succeeded by Archbishop Abbott	ib.
His Leniency to the Nonconformists	ib.
Character of this reign in its religious aspect	47
Death of James	48
Was succeeded by his son Charles	ib.
The Puritans expected countenance from the new King, who was accompanied on his journey to London to assume the crown by Dr. Preston, head of their party	ib.
Their Disappointment	ib.
Charles's Bigotry and Intolerance	ib.
Was influenced by his Primate Laud	49
Attempts for a Union with Rome	ib.
Persecution of the Puritans	50

CONTENTS.   ix

	PAGES.
Sufferings of Burton, Prynne, Bastwick, and Dr. Leighton	50
Depression of the Puritans from the Persecution of Charles and Laud	51
They cogitated Emigration to America	ib.
Extent of the Puritan Emigration thither in Twelve Years of Laud's Administration	52
The King issued an Order in Council restraining further Emigration	53
Consequences of this Order	ib.
Hampden, Pym, Cromwell and Hazelrigg were prevented emigrating	ib.
Effects Fatal to Charles and Laud	ib.
Despotic character of Charles in the Civil Administration of his kingdom	54
Resistance of the Puritans	ib.
Subsequent War disastrous to the King	55
Consequences of the National Conquest	ib.
Monarchy Ceased	ib.
The High Commission Court and Star Chamber were Abolished	ib.
Episcopacy was Disestablished	ib.
Complete Religious Liberty Granted	ib.
Presbyterianism and Independency the two dominant Sects	56
Their respective Leaders	ib.
The former stronger in Parliament, the latter in the Army	56–57
Aided by the Scottish Army, Presbyterianism is allied to the State	ib.
Intolerant Proceedings of the new Ally	ib.
Ascendancy of Cromwell and the Army	57
Independency became the State Religion	ib.

	PAGES.
Contrast between Presbyterianism and Independency as State Allies	57
Independency completely Tolerant	57–58
Testimony of Mr. Hume on the point	58
Rise of the Quakers	ib.
Birth, Character and Doctrines of George Fox, their Founder	59
Narrative of their early Proceedings	ib.
Death of Cromwell	60
His Character	ib.
State of Religion during the Commonwealth	63–64
Eminent Theologians of the Period	64–65
The Sceptre wrested from Cromwell's son and successor, Richard	65
Charles the Second ascended the Throne	ib.
The Restoration	ib.
Its Character	ib.
The King by his Declaration of Breda guaranteed complete Religious Toleration	66
He violated his Promise	ib.
Caused to be passed the Act of Uniformity	ib.
Consequences of the Act	67
On St. Bartholomew's Day, 1662, Two Thousand Ministers of the Established Church resigned their livings, rather than conform to the Act	ib.
The name Puritan was exchanged for Nonconformist	68
It comprised Presbyterians, Independents, Baptists, and Quakers	ib.
The Act of Uniformity increased their number	ib.
Passing of the Act of 1665 to punish the Nonconformist Clergy	ib.
The Conventicle Act, 1670	69
Its severe Provisions	ib.

CONTENTS. xi

	PAGES.
Consequences of these Acts	70
Trial by Jury taken away from Persons accused of violating the Acts	ib.
The King, to favour the Papists, to whom he was much inclined, published a Declaration of Indulgence to all Religious Sects, and suspended the Penal Laws	71
Passing of the Test Act	ib.
Consequences of the Act	ib.
It excluded numerous Dissenters from public offices	ib.
Charles was succeeded by his brother James	73
James avowed himself a Papist	ib.
Sent an Emissary to the Pope proposing the re-admission of England into the Romish Church	74
The Sagacious Pontiff neglected the Offer	ib.
James's Hostility to all the Protestant Sects	ib.
Attempted to re-establish the High Commission Court	75
The King issued an Ecclesiastical Commission, with unlimited power over the Protestant Church of England	ib.
The King's design was to suppress Protestantism and raise Popery into supremacy	ib.
Inconsistency of James	ib.
He suspended all Penal Laws, and granted Liberty of Conscience to all his subjects	ib.
The King's design was to protect the Papists, but Nonconformists equally enjoyed its benefits	76
Hostility of Churchmen and Papists, the Rival Sects	ib.
Nonconformists held aloof	ib.
James sent the Earl of Castlemaine, his Ambassador, to the Pope to negotiate the Reunion of his kingdom with Rome	77

CONTENTS.

	PAGES.
The Pontiff discouraged the proposal	77
The King's patronage of Roman Catholics	78
James in 1688 published a Second Declaration of Indulgence of all Religions.	ib.
Commanded the Royal Order to be read in every Established Church immediately after Divine Service	ib.
Resistance of the Clergy	79
Six Prelates petitioned the King against the Royal Order	ib.
James committed the remonstrating Bishops to the Tower	ib.
Trial of the Bishops and their Acquittal	ib.
Alarm of Churchmen, Nonconformists, and the Nation at the Popish Encroachments and Arbitrary Proceedings of James	ib.
They invited William, Prince of Orange, to ascend the British Throne	80
The Prince of Orange accepted the Invitation	ib.
He issued a Proclamation of full Religious Liberty	81
William landed at Torbay in 1688	ib.
Multitudes joined his Standard	ib.
James was deserted by his Army, and he retired to France	ib.
The Revolution	ib.
William and Mary were placed on the British Throne	81–82
Character of William	82
His Religious and Political Views liberal	ib.
Royal Address to the Parliament	83
Motion made to abolish the Sacramental Test for public office	ib.
Motion lost, though sanctioned by their Majesties	ib.

CONTENTS.   xiii

	PAGES.
The King caused to be introduced a clause that receiving the Sacrament in the Church of England or in any Protestant Place of Worship within a Year before or after the Admission into Public Office should be a sufficient Qualification	83
Clause rejected by Parliament	84
William's further efforts for the relief of Nonconformists	ib.
The Bill for a Comprehension of all Protestant Sects	ib.
Passed the House of Lords	85
The Commons neglected the Bill, and in lieu thereof they presented an Address to their Majesties, thanking them for their gracious Declaration, and praying them to issue writs convening a Convocation of the Clergy to deliberate on ecclesiastical matters, and to give ease to Protestant Dissenters	ib.
The King's Answer	86
He granted a Commission to the Bishops and twenty Dignitaries of the Church of England to prepare such alterations of the Liturgy and Canons, with proposals for the Reformation of the Ecclesiastical Courts, as might most conduce to the edification and uniting of the Church, and tend to reconcile all differences among their Majesties' Protestant subjects	ib.
Outcry against the Commission, which became fruitless	87
The King persevered in his efforts for the relief of his Nonconformist subjects	88
The Bill " to exempt their Majesties' Protestant subjects dissenting from the Church of England from the Penalties of certain laws "	ib.

CONTENTS.

	PAGES.
Passed both Houses of Parliament	88
Received the Royal Assent 24th May, 1689	ib.
Provisions of the Act	ib.
Relieves Protestant Dissenters from the penal statutes	ib.
Consequences of the relieving Act	89
Death of William	90
Succeeded by Anne, daughter of James the Second	ib.
Her Hostility to the Nonconformists	91
Stimulated by the Hierarchy	ib.
The Bill to prevent Occasional Conformity	92
Its extreme provisions	93
Passed the Commons	94
Was violently opposed by the Lords	ib.
They introduced considerable Amendments	ib.
The Commons refused the Amendments	ib.
The Bill lost	ib.
The Bill to prevent Occasional Conformity introduced to the Commons in a milder form the next session	95
Passed the Commons	ib.
Rejected by the Lords	ib.
The Bill introduced to the Commons the following session	ib.
Passed the Commons	ib.
Rejected by the Lords	ib.
No attempt made for several years to reintroduce the Bill to prevent Occasional Conformity	96

The Earl of Nottingham, a deserter from the Tories to the Whigs, introduced to the Lords the principle of the Bill against Occasional Conformity, under the specious title of "An Act for preserving the Protestant Religion by better securing

	PAGES.
the Church of England, and for continuing the toleration granted to Protestant Dissenters by an Act for supplying the defects thereof".	96
Passed the Lords and Commons, and the Queen, who approved the Bill, gave it her willing assent.	97
Bill to prevent Children receiving Instruction unless it inculcated the doctrines of the Church of England, passed the Commons and Lords, and received the Royal Assent	ib.
The Queen died on the 1st of August, 1719, being the day upon which the last mentioned Act, called the Schism Act, was to have come into operation, whereupon its provisions were never enforced	99
Steady increase of Nonconformity during the reign of Queen Anne, notwitstanding the severity of the measures passed for its suppression	100
The Brunswick Royal Family then ascended the British Throne	101
The Tories supplanted by the Whigs	102
George the First was favourable to the Nonconformists	ib.
They presented him with Addresses of congratulation on his Accession	ib.
Act passed making permanent the Act of William and Mary, substituting a solemn Declaration for an Oath in the case of Quakers	ib.
Bill to repeal the Occasional Conformity and Schism Acts under the title of "An Act for strengthening the Protestant interest in these Kingdoms," passed both Houses of Parliament, and became law on the 18th February, 1719	104

	PAGES.

Bill for the Suppression of Blasphemy and Profaneness, designed chiefly against Nonconformists, introduced to the Peers, but rejected . . . 105
Steady progress of Nonconformity during this reign 107
Death of George the First 108
His son, George the Second, ascended the throne . 109
The King favourable to Civil and Religious Liberty ib.
Convocation of the Clergy attempted to pass Measures coercive of Religious Liberty, but they were suppressed by the King . . . ib.
Act passed compelling the Clergy to adopt summary proceedings before Magistrates for the recovery of Tithes and Churchrates from Quakers 111
Countenanced by the King, Nonconformists attempted, but unsuccessfully, to procure a repeal of the Test Acts 112
Rise of John Wesley, founder of Wesleyan Methodism . . . . ib.
Assisted by his brother Charles, and by George Whitefield, the founder of Calvinistic Methodism 113
Ardour and Success of their Ministry . . . ib.
Death of George the Second . . . . . ib.
Succeeded by his Grandson, George the Third, who was favourable to Religious Liberty . . . ib.
Significant Petition to Parliament from several hundred Ministers and numerous lay members of the Established Church, asserting the right of private judgment in the interpretation of the Scriptures . . . . ib.
Act passed relieving Nonconformist Ministers and Laymen from subscribing to the obnoxious Articles prescribed by the Toleration Act . . 114

CONTENTS. xvii

	PAGES.
The severe Laws passed in former reigns against Roman Catholics	115
Act passed for their Repeal	ib.
Insidious but abortive attempt of Lord Sidmouth against Nonconformist preaching	ib.
Opposed successfully by the whole Dissenting community, and denounced by many of the Peers	116
Death of George the Third	ib.
Accession of George the Fourth	ib.
Act passed repealing the Corporation and Test Acts	ib.
Act passed to relieve Roman Catholics of their religious and political Disabilities	117
Death of George the Fourth and Accession of William the Fourth	118
The Act legalizing Marriages in Nonconformist places of worship	ib.
Extensively adopted by Dissenters	ib.
Death of William the Fourth	ib.
Accession of our good and gracious Queen Victoria	ib.
Her prosperous reign over a contented nation	ib.
Gave her cordial and gracious assent to every Act passed by Parliament, erasing from the Statute Book the odious laws enacted during the Tudor and Stuart reigns against Religious Liberty	119
For the removal of:	
Jewish disabilities, in 1858 and 1860	ib.
The last remains of the Test and Corporation Acts, in 1866	ib.
Compulsory Churchrates, in 1868	ib.
Religious Tests in the Universities, in 1871	ib.
Present civil and religious condition of the Nonconformists	ib.

CHAPTER II.

THE LAWS RELATING TO PUBLIC WORSHIP.

PAGES.

Gifts for religious and charitable uses and purposes had become so general that the Legislature passed the Act 9 George II., cap. 36, to restrain them 123

After 24th June, 1736, no land or other hereditaments, or money, or other personal estate, to be invested in the purchase of land or other hereditaments, should be given or conveyed to any person or persons, body politic or corporate, or otherwise, for any estate or interest whatsoever, unless such gift or conveyance should be made by deed, executed in the presence of two or more credible witnesses, twelve calendar months before the death of such donor or grantor, including the days of the execution and death, and be enrolled in the Court of Chancery within six calendar months next after the execution thereof, and unless stocks in the public funds should be transferred six calendar months before the death of the donor or grantor, including the days of the transfer and death, and unless the same should be made to take effect in possession for the charitable use

CONTENTS.

intended, immediately from the making thereof, and be without any power of revocation, reservation, trust, condition, limitation or agreement whatsoever for the benefit of the donor or grantor, or of any person or persons claiming under him. Section 1	124
Exception of purchases for full and valuable consideration. Section 2	ib.
All gifts and grants made in any other manner than by that Act directed should be absolutely void. Section 3	125
Section 2 was explained, by a subsequent Act, not to except purchases for full valuable consideration *entirely* from the operation of the Mortmain Act: 9 George IV., cap. 85	ib.
The statute last mentioned confirmed all purchases and conveyances for valuable consideration made prior thereto for charitable uses taking immediate effect in possession, which had not been already annulled or were the subject of legal contention at its passing	ib.
"Charitable use" held to comprise every *public* religious, philanthropic, or benevolent object .	126
But not a *private* charity	ib.
The Statute of Mortmain extends to land of copyhold tenure	ib.
The conveyance for a religious or charitable use must take effect immediately	ib.
If its operation be postponed for any period long or short, or if it contain any reservation of a portion of the property in quantity or interest, or any use or trust declared or benefit reserved in favour of the grantor, it is void	ib.

	PAGES.
Exception of a demise for any term of years, if made to take effect for the charitable use, and the term to commence in possession, within one year from the date of the deed	127
Rack rent or other annual payment of full value declared equivalent to a sum of money actually paid	ib.
A declaration or trust that the grantor's tomb shall be repaired by the grantee will not render void a conveyance of land for a religious use . .	ib.
Secus a trust for the perpetual repair of a monument in the church	ib.
Reservation by the grantor of power to appoint the minister or pastor of a chapel, or to make further direction for its management, will not render the conveyance void	128
If the conveyance be void for non-compliance with the provisions of the Mortmain Act, the grantor, or his heir at law, may take advantage of the defect, and recover the property by action .	ib.
Execution of the conveyance by the grantor alone before its enrolment sufficient, and its retention by him immaterial	ib.
The Court will not presume its enrolment . .	ib.
Section 1 of the Mortmain Act held to apply to the first or original deed of conveyance for a religious or charitable use only	129
Every subsequent disposition of property already in mortmain sufficient if executed by ordinary deed, as a conveyance to new trustees . .	ib.
To bring the conveyance within the exception of the second section of the Mortmain Act, the consideration money must be paid to the grantor	

by the person or persons for whose benefit it is made	130
If the religious or charitable uses be declared by a deed separate from the conveyance, the first mentioned alone requires enrolment	ib.
A gift by will, of land, or of any estate, term or interest in it, including leasehold, or of any rent, profit, or easement out of land, for a religious or charitable use, is void	131
A gift by will, of money charged upon or payable out of land, is void. As, of the proceeds of the sale of land; or of money due on mortgage legal or equitable of, or being a lien on, land; or owing on the security of turnpike tolls, or of the poor or county rates; or a judgment debt registered against the land of the debtor	132
Money bonds charged on the police rates of a county, held by Jessel, M. R., to be pure personalty	ib.
Bequest of the unpaid purchase money due on the sale of land, or on the sale of the growing crop of land, invalid	133
A bequest of money charged on the rates and tolls raised under an Act of Parliament for improving the navigation of a river not thereby declared to be considered as personal estate is void, as also of a mortgage of the "works, rents, and rates," under a Town's Improvement Act	ib.
A bqeuest of the *future* rent of land for a religious or charitable use is invalid, but of rent in arrear is good	ib.
A bequest of the interest of a mortgage of land due, or to become due, is void	ib.

c

CONTENTS.

	PAGES.
A bequest of money to redeem land belonging to a charity, from a mortgage or lien, is invalid	133
A bequest of pure personalty for a religious or charitable use is void, if the object be to secure to it the possession or enjoyment of land	135
A gift by will of money due on a policy of assurance for a religious or charitable use is good, although the company's assets include real property which is liable to pay the sum assured	ib.
Generally shares in joint stock companies are not interests in land within the prohibition of the Mortmain Act, whether the Act by which they are incorporated does or does not contain a clause that the shares shall be deemed to be personal estate, and if given by will for a religious or charitable use the bequest is valid: *e.g.*	
Shares in a gas company;	
Or in a canal company;	
Or in a dock company;	
Or in a railway company.	
Excepting in any of the cases the share or interest bequeathed should, in the ordinary course of events, vest specifically in the holder thereof a portion of the land	136
Gift of 3½ per cent. stock in the Metropolitan Board of Works held void	ib.
The debentures of a railway or other company, executed in the mortgage form of the undertaking pursuant to the Companies Clauses Consolidation Act, 1845, Schedule C, may be given by will for a religious or charitable use	ib.
A gift by will of money to be applied wholly in erecting, enlarging or improving a church,	

CONTENTS.   xxiii

PAGES.

chapel, or building standing or being on land already in mortmain, is good 137

If the testator direct the erection of a church, chapel, school or other building, to render the bequest valid he must specify the land already in mortmain on which it is to be built . . . . *ib.*

A bequest of money for the erection or repair of a church, chapel, or building on land already in mortmain, or for the endowment of churches or chapels in existence, is valid . . . . *ib.*

Where a testator directed his charity legacies to be paid out of his pure personalty, the specialty creditors were ordered to be paid out of the real estate, to ensure the former 138

A devise or bequest for a religious or charitable use rendered void by the Statute of Mortmain lapses to the heir at law, or nearest of kin, of the testator according to its quality, or sinks into his residuary estate . . . . *ib.*

Mitigating statutes . . . . *ib.*

All persons may by will, duly executed three months at least before death, bequeath all their estate, not exceeding in the case of each testator, in real property five acres, or in personalty £500 in value, for erecting, rebuilding, repairing, purchasing, or providing any church or chapel where the Liturgy of the Church of England shall be used, or any mansion house for the residence of a minister of the Church of England officiating in such church or chapel, or any outbuildings, churchyard, or glebe for the same respectively . . . . *ib.*

A gift exceeding five acres or £500 may, on petition

	PAGES
to the Lord Chancellor, be ordered to be reduced to either limit: 48 George III., cap. 108	139
Any person or persons being seised or entitled in fee simple, fee tail, or for life or lives, of or to any land of freehold tenure, having the beneficial interest therein, and being in possession thereof, may grant, convey, or enfranchise by way of gift, sale, or exchange in fee simple or for any term of years, any quantity not exceeding one acre of such land, not being part of a demesne or pleasure ground attached to a mansion, as a site for a church, chapel, meeting house, or other place of Divine worship, or for the residence of a minister officiating in such place of worship, or in any place of worship within one mile of such site, or for a burial place; or any number of such sites, provided each does not exceed one acre	ib.
Conveyance may be in the form therein set forth, to the execution of which by each party thereto one witness shall be sufficient, and shall be valid notwithstanding the death of the donor or grantor within twelve calendar months from such execution	140
The same powers extended to copyhold land if the provisions of the Lands Clauses Consolidation Act, 1845, should be observed: 36 and 37 Victoria, cap. 50	ib.
Semble the powers granted by the last mentioned Act are confined to a conveyance of land, and do not extend to a rent, profit, or easement out of land	ib.
Reference to other mitigating statutes	141

CONTENTS. XXV

PAGES.

The chapel or place of worship must be certified and registered, to entitle it and the congregation, together with the minister or preacher, to the protection of the statutes in that behalf . . . 142

Any person or persons who shall wilfully and maliciously or contemptuously disturb any meeting or congregation of persons assembled for religious worship, permitted or authorised by that or any former Act, or shall in any way molest or insult any preacher, teacher, or person officiating thereat, or any person or persons there present, shall upon proof thereof before a justice of the peace by two or more credible witnesses, find two sureties to be bound by recognizances in the sum of £50 to answer for such offence, and in default to remain till the next General or Quarter Sessions, and upon conviction shall suffer the penalty of £40: 52 George III., cap. 155, section 12 . . . 143

Each defendant is liable under this statute, on conviction, to the penalty of £40 . . . . *ib.*

Provisions of the last mentioned Act with respect to registration of the chapel or meeting house . *ib.*

Every person knowingly permitting or suffering any congregation or assembly for religious worship of Protestants or (now) Roman Catholics, or Jews, or any other body or denomination, where more than twenty persons, besides the inmates of the house, shall be present, to meet in any place occupied by him until the same shall be certified and registered as therein mentioned, shall on conviction thereof before two or more justices of the peace forfeit and pay not more than £20, nor

	PAGES
less than £1, for every time such congregation or assembly should meet. Section 2 . . .	144
Any person teaching or preaching in any congregation or assembly as mentioned in Section 2, in any place, without the consent of the occupier thereof, shall on conviction before two or more justices forfeit and pay not more than £30, nor less than £2. Section 3	145
Every person teaching or preaching as aforesaid, who should refuse to attend to take the oaths and make the declarations mentioned in Sections 4 and 5, or before taking and making the same, shall on conviction before two or more justices forfeit and pay not more than £10 nor less than 10s. Section 5	ib.
Every person teaching or preaching as aforesaid at any meeting with the door bolted, or barred, or otherwise fastened so as to prevent any person entering therein during the time of such meeting, shall on conviction in the same way forfeit and pay not more than £20, nor less than £2. Section 11	ib.
All teachers and preachers shall be exempt from the penalty imposed by Section 5 if they shall, when thereunto required by a justice of the peace, take the oaths and make the declarations prescribed by law. Sections 4 and 5. . .	ib.
Nothing contained in any previous Act of Parliament shall apply to the following : (18 and 19 Victoria, cap. 86).	146

1. To any congregation or assembly for religious worship held in any parish or any ecclesiastical district, and conducted by the Incumbent, or if

the Incumbent be non-resident, by the Curate of such parish or district, or by any person authorised by them respectively	146
2. To any congregation or assembly for religious worship meeting in a private dwelling house or on the premises belonging thereto . . .	*ib.*
3. To any congregation or assembly for religious worship, meeting occasionally in any building not usually appropriated to religious worship .	147
No person permitting any such congregation or assembly to meet in any such place occupied by him as last aforesaid shall be liable to any penalty for so doing	*ib.*
Provisions of 18 and 19 Victoria, cap. 81, with respect to the registration of chapels and places of religious worship, after the 30th July, 1855	*ib.*

Any person who shall be guilty of riotous, violent, or indecent behaviour in any cathedral church, parish or district church, or chapel of the Church of England, or in any place of worship duly certified under 18 and 19 Victoria, cap. 81, whether during the celebration of Divine worship or at any other time, or in any churchyard or burial ground, or who shall molest or misuse any preacher duly authorised to preach therein, or any clergyman in holy orders, ministering or celebrating any sacrament, or any Divine service, rite or office in any cathedral church or chapel, or in any churchyard or burial ground, shall on conviction thereof before two or more justices of the peace be liable to a penalty not exceeding £5, or at the discretion of the justices to imprisonment not exceeding two calendar months: 23 and 24 Victoria, cap. 32, section 2 . . . 149

Whosoever shall, by threat or force, obstruct or prevent, or endeavour to obstruct or prevent, any clergyman or other minister in or from celebrating Divine service, or otherwise officiating in any church, chapel, or meeting house, or other place of Divine worship, or in or from the performance of his duty in the lawful burial of the dead in any churchyard or other burial place, or shall strike or offer any violence to, or shall upon any civil process or under the pretence of executing any civil process, arrest any clergyman or other minister who is engaged in, or to the knowledge of the offender is about to engage in, any of the rites or duties in that section mentioned, or who to the knowledge of the offender shall be going to perform the same or returning therefrom, shall be guilty of a misdemeanour, and shall be liable on conviction to imprisonment not exceeding two years with or without hard labour, and in addition to or in lieu thereof, the Court may fine the offender and require him to enter into recognizance, with or without sureties, to keep the peace and be of good behaviour for not exceeding one year: 24 and 25 Victoria, cap. 100, section 36 . . *ib.*

Provisions of the Act 6 and 7 William IV., cap. 85, entitled "An Act for Marriages in England," with respect to registering chapels or other places of religious worship for solemnizing marriages therein 150

CASES CITED.

	PAGES.
Alexander v. Brame, 7 Jurist N. S., 889	133
Arnold v. Chapman, 1 Vesey Senior, 108	126, 135, 138
Ashton v. Jones, 16 Jurist N. S., 970	129
Ashworth v. Munn, L. J. Ch., 747	132
Attorney-General v. Bishop of Chester, 1 Brown C. C., 444	137
Attorney-General v. Caldwell, Amb., 635	132
Attorney-General v. Davies, 9 Vesey, 535	135, 137
Attorney-General v. Graves, Amb., 155	132
Attorney-General v. Hodgson, 15 Simons, 146	135
Attorney-General v. Hull, 9 Hare, 647	135
Attorney-General v. Hyde, 2 Amb., 750	137
Attorney-General v. Lord Mountmorris, 1 Dick, 379	138
Attorney-General v. Meyrick, 2 Vesey Senior, 44	132
Attorney-General v. Munby, 1 Mer., 327	128, 129, 137
Attorney-General v. Nash, 3 Brown C. C., 526	137
Attorney-General v. Tomkins, Ambl., 216	131
Attorney-General v. Tyndall, 2 Eden, 207; S. C. Ambl., 614	131
Attorney-General v. Weymouth, Ambl. 20	132
Attree v. Hawe, 9 Ch. D., 337	136
Brook v. Badley, L. R. 3, C. A., 672	133
Bunting v. Marriott, 19 Beavan, 163	135
Cadbury v. Smith, L. R. 9 Equity, 37	133
Chandler v. Howell, 4 Ch. D., 651	133
In re Clark, 1 Ch. D., 497	126
Cluff v. Cluff, 2 Ch. D., 222	136
Colluson v. Pater, 2 Russell and Mylne, 344	132

CONTENTS.

	PAGES.
Cook v. Stationers' Company, 3 Mylne and Keene, 262	138
Corbyn v. French, 4 Vesey, 418	134
Cox v. Davie, 7 Ch. D., 204	137
Dixon v. Baker, 3 Young & C., 677	139
Doe d. Howson v. Waterton, 3 Barnewall & Alderson, 149	126, 129
Doe d. Preece v. Howells, 2 Barnewall & Adolphus, 744	128, 130
Doe d. Thompson v. Pitcher, 3 Maule & Selwyn, 407	127
Doe d. Wellard v. Hawthorn, 2 Barnewall & Alderson, 96	128, 131
Doe v. Copestake, 6 East, 328	126
Doe v. Wright, 2 Barnewall & Alderson, 710	128
Edwards v. Hall, 11 Hare, 13; 6 De Gex, M. and G., 599	133, 136, 137
Entwisle v. Davies, L. R. 4 Equity, 272	136
Finch v. Squire, 10 Vesey, 41	132
Fisher v. Brierley, 1 De Gex, F. & J., 643	128, 137
Foy v. Foy, 1 Cox, 165	137
Gibbs v. Rumsey, 2 Vesey & B., 294	138
Giblett v. Hobson, 5 Simons, 651; 3 M. and K., 517	137
Glubb v. Attorney-General, Ambl. 373	137
Grieves v. Case, 2 Cox, 301; 4 Brown, C. C., 67	128
Harris v. Barnes, Amb. 651	137
Harris v. Du Pasquier, 26 L. T., 689	126
Harrison v. Harrison, 1 Russell & Mylne, 71	133
Hayter v. Tucker, 4 K. & J., 243	136
Henchman v. Attorney-General, 3 Mylne and Keene, 485	138
Hoare v. Osborne, 1 L. R. Equity, 585	128
Holdsworth v. Davenport, L. R. 3 Ch. D., 185	136
Hone v. Medcraft, 1 Brown C. C., 261	132
House v. Chapman, 4 Vesey, 542	138

Ion v. Ashton, 28 Beavan, 379	132
Jacson v. Governors of Queen Anne's Bounty, 43 L. T. Rep. N. S., 116	132
Johnston v. Swann, 3 Maddox, 467	132
Knapp v. Williams, 4 Vesey, 430	132
Lambrey v. Gurr, 6 Maddox, 151	126
Langstaff v. Remuson, 1 Drewry, 28	135
Lewis v. Allenby, 10 L. R. Eq., 668	128
Lloyd v. Lloyd, 2 Simons N. S., 255	127
Marsh v. Attorney-General, 5 Beavan, 433	135
Mitchell v. Moberly, 3 Ch. D., 655	136
Morice v. Bishop of Durham, 9 Vesey, 399; 10 Vesey, 522	126
Morris v. Glyn, 27 Beavan, 218	136
Myers v. Perigal, 2 De Gex, M. & G., 599	136
Paice v. Archbishop of Canterbury, 14 Vesey, 368	132
Pickering v. Lord Stamford, 2 Vesey Junior, 272, 581	132
Poor v. Mial, Mad. & G., 32	135
Pritchard v. Arbouin, 3 Russell C. C., 456	137
R. v. Cheere, 4 Barnewall & Cresswell, 902	143
R. v. Hube, 5 Term Reports, 542	143
Shanley v. Baker, 4 Vesey, 732	131
Symons v. Marine Society, 2 Giff., 325	132
Taylor v. Lindley, 2 De Gex, F. & G., 599	136
Walker v. Richardson, T. T., 1837; Exchequer, 2, Meeson & Welsby, 882	129
Waterhouse v. Holmes, 2 Simons, 162	132, 135
Webley v. Dobson, 4 Russell, 342	137
White v. Evans, 4 Vesey, 21	132
Wickham v. Marquis of Bath, 11 Jurist N. S., 988	126
Wright v. Smithies, 10 East, 409	129

STATUTES CITED.

	PAGES.
30 Car. II., c. 2	146
1 William & Mary, c. 1	146
1 William & Mary, c. 18	146
9 George II., c. 36	123
19 George III., c. 44	146
48 George III., c. 108	138
52 George III., c. 155	143
9 George IV., c. 85	125
2 & 3 William IV., c. 115	144
6 & 7 William IV., c. 85	150
9 & 10 Victoria, c. 59	144
18 & 19 Victoria, c. 81	147
18 & 19 Victoria, c. 86	146
23 & 24 Victoria, c. 32	149
24 & 25 Victoria, c. 100	149
26 & 27 Victoria, c. 106	127

STATUTES PRINTED VERBATIM IN APPENDIX.

	PAGES.
4 & 5 Victoria (1841), cap. 38, entitled "An Act to afford further Facilities for the Conveyance and Endowment of Sites for Schools"	157
13 & 14 Victoria (1850), cap. 28, entitled "An Act to render more simple and effectual the Titles by which Congregations or Societies for purposes of Religious Worship or Education in England and Ireland hold property for such purposes"	158
24 Victoria (1861), cap. 9, entitled "An Act to amend the Law relating to the Conveyance of Land for Charitable Uses"	163
25 Victoria (1862), cap. 17, entitled "An Act to extend the Time for making Enrolments under the Act passed in the last session of Parliament, 24 Victoria, cap. 9"	169
27 Victoria (1864), cap. 13, entitled "An Act to further extend the Time for making Enrolments under the Act 24 Victoria, cap. 9, and otherwise to amend the said Law"	171
29 & 30 Victoria (1866), cap. 57, entitled "An Act to make further provision for the Enrolment of certain Deeds, Assurances, and other Instruments relating to Charitable Uses"	174

31 & 32 Victoria (1868), cap. 44, entitled "An Act for facilitating the Acquisition and Enjoyment of sites for Buildings for Religious, Educational, Literary, Scientific, and other Charitable Purposes" 177

33 & 34 Victoria (1870), cap. 34, entitled "An Act to amend the Law as to the Investment on Real Securities of Trust Funds held for Public and Charitable Purposes". 179

34 Victoria (1871), cap. 13, entitled "An Act to facilitate Gifts of Land for Public Parks, Schools, and Museums" 180

36 & 37 Victoria (1873), cap. 50, entitled "An Act to afford further Facilities for the Conveyance of Land for Sites for Places of Religious Worship and for Burial places" 183

38 & 39 Victoria (1875), cap. 68, entitled "An Act for making further Provision respecting the Department of Science and Art" 188

FORMS.

(1.)

Deed of Conveyance of a Freehold Site for a Wesleyan Methodist Chapel (with declaration of trusts by reference to the Model Deed) 191

(2.)

Trusts of a Congregational Chapel Deed . . 195

(3.)

Trusts of a Baptist Chapel Deed . . . 207

(4.)

Trusts of a Calvinistic Methodist Chapel Deed . 210

THE RISE AND PROGRESS OF RELIGIOUS LIBERTY IN ENGLAND.

CHAPTER I.

THOSE who have attempted dominion over the mind have in all ages been much more numerous than they who have merely attempted to enslave the body. Their policy has been also the wiser, for by it they have essayed to wrest from man the only weapon of successful resistance against tyranny, to extinguish the light by the aid of which he would see the hideousness of its mien.

The history of the world hitherto presents one alternation of slavish subjection to authority, and of struggles for emancipation from the yoke. In the one case we see the omnipotent influence of mind in chaining whole nations, and even continents, in a worse than Egyptian bondage; in the other we witness the resistless power of the same agent in bursting the fetters, and establishing the birthright independence of man. In no department of life have these conflicting achievements of mind been more remarkable than in that of religion. In none have we witnessed more degrading or long continued, thraldom; in none have been seen more glorious struggles to be free. On no field has liberty been more signally defeated, and human nature laid prostrate; on none has the battle of truth been more valiantly fought. Religion presents many advantages for the tyrant's success. She presents him with weapons which cannot be found in the world besides; he draws his influence from sources which are beyond the terrestrial experience of man. That great futurity which lies beyond this life's span, with its capabilities for raising hopes and producing fears, are at his command. Denunciations more awful than the cataract, threats more terrific than thunder, with invitations sweeter and more delightful than the summer warblings of the grove, are at his bidding. He appeals to the tenderest and most susceptible part of man, his religious nature. He holds the wand whose influence is magical over the human heart. The success of the religious tyrant has therefore been as frequent as his reign has been long continued. No spot of the habitable earth but has bowed to the despot's sway; none but for ages has groaned beneath his blighting yoke.

The theatre on which have been witnessed religious thraldom the most humiliating, and emancipation the most glorious, was Europe. For ages prior to the sixteenth century, the mind of Europe bowed to one despot's power; its cogitations assumed the righteousness of the yoke. The bondage was shared in common by monarch and mechanic, peer and peasant, lord and vassal. Even the philosopher in his scholastic musings does not appear to have questioned the authority; philosophy itself bore an impress of the tyrant's sway. Whatsoever light, showing the illegality of the power, the man of science may in his ruminations have met, for some cause or other, either indifference or dread, he transmitted not the light to the world, but carried it with him to the tomb. It may be that many a mind did see the enormity of the claim, and many a breast did burn with the ire of conscious wrong, but that the awe of the "powers that were" repressed the insurrection, and confined the tumult within the circle of their own breasts. It is possible that, could we enter the murky regions of the grave, and scan the thoughts and feelings which once animated the now mighty dead, many a Luther in thought would be found prior to the sixteenth century; and who, had they possessed the ardour of that fiery soul, would ages before have blessed the world with the Reformation's freedom and light.

But howsoever that may be, and it is a question solvable by the Omniscient alone, the fact like a bold promontory stands out in the history of the world, that Europe for ages prior to the century in question lay prostrate at the feet of Rome; that its counsels, its laws, its judgments and decrees, were impregnated with the papal sway. With devout submission she obeyed the tyrant's commands, with terror she regarded his frowns, with rapture his smiles. His favour was her life, his anger her death. At his bidding monarchs were hurled off their thrones; by his command the myriad masses were chained in the dust, and all with murmurless submission bowed to the edict nor dared whisper an appeal. The minds of peasant and philosopher appear to have regarded with equal veneration the papal chair; its foundation was Divine, its power was absolute and uncontrollable. She thus deified man, uplifting human nature to the throne of Divinity, she invested frail man with the sceptre of Heaven; elevating humanity to a dominion so lofty, she stripped the Godhead of His righteous prerogative, and conferred it on a being, finite, mortal and weak! The error was great, the sin grievous, and the penalty she dearly paid. This was no other than the blood of her people, which for ages streamed through her valleys and plains; the drainage of her wealth; the benighting of her mental and moral horizon; and the prostration of her liberty. This is the spectacle which Europe presents to the eye of the historian prior to the sixteenth century. But the night of bondage was not to endure for ever; a day was to dawn, a sun to arise.

In the order of that providence which superintends the operations of this world, it has happened that the mightiest achievements have been effected by agents the least likely for the enterprise; that the greatest changes have been accomplished by instrumentality apparently the most unequal to the task. It appears as though the Author of that providence wanted on occasions to confound the wisdom of men, and on others perhaps to demonstrate the vastness of those capabilities with which He has endowed man. In the beginning of the sixteenth century, and within the walls of a convent at Erfurt in Germany, an individual might be seen humbly and quietly performing the duties of his order, which were those of an Augustinian monk. There was nought in his appearance to distinguish him from the crowd of priests that surrounded him, and with equal alacrity and subjection his priestly duties were performed. But beneath an undistinguished exterior was hid a soul of fire, within was a spirit equal to the loftiest deeds. Probably also at this time, when immured obscurely within the convent bounds, his mind brooded over those great enterprises which at no distant period would rivet the attention of the world, shake Europe to its centre, and rend the foundation of the Vatican itself. It may be that at this period a rude outline of that glorious yet perilous career which he was destined afterwards to run was sketched, although doubtless in its course consequences and contingencies which he never contemplated followed, and others which he had ardently wished for never came to pass.

This was Martin Luther. The papal power had in his time reached its zenith, its abominations had no less attained their maturity. The sovereigns of Europe were so many instruments in the hand of a religious despot, their crowns trembled at his nod, their thrones tottered beneath his frown. The people were equally subjugated to his authority; they looked at the hand which bound them, with the same religious awe. Sovereigns and people, rulers and ruled, nobles and commons, equally reverenced the tyrant's sway; and well did he understand his power: it ministered as much to his profit as pleasure; it was found as efficient a means for replenishing an exhausted exchequer as for supplying the cravings of an ambitious mind. No better means could be devised for satisfying the demands of avarice than to vend to human nature the right to do wrong, the liberty of pursuing its evil inclinations without being amenable to the court of Heaven. No commodity ever commanded so high a price, even the revenues of kingdoms were insignificant compared with that derived from this source. The commodity was also of universal demand; it was needed as much by peer as peasant, the rich as the poor, for all had the same nature, and felt the same desire to infringe with impunity the laws of the Most High; and this was freely advertised. Nor was the right sparingly exercised. No part of Christendom but received absolution from sin, none but enjoyed the liberty of transgressing without penalty the law of their God. But neither was gratuitous; it was sold for a price, and that consisted of earthly coin. The Pope's exchequer was filled by the poor man's copper equally with the rich man's gold; the stream whereby the reservoir was supplied descended from all ranks and all countries alike. It was thus that man attempted to sell the sceptre of Heaven, to barter the righteousness of the Most High; it was thus that he attempted to compromise the throne of the skies.

As a natural consequence, in this age all manner of sin and licentiousness unblushingly prevailed, the floodgates of passion were opened, and their torrents deluged the world. The checks of religion and the restraints of morality were loosened. Crime was general, because pardonable; sin was universal, because absolvable. Morality was practised only because convenient, the voice of eternal justice was hushed by the lullaby of the priest. Religion was but a mass of pompous forms and gorgeous ceremonies, an empty shell, a body without life. Right and wrong, truth and error, were the mere reflection of the Pontiff's mind, and as changeable as the chameleon's hue. The Book of Life was banished from the languages of men, its precious truths were concealed in the mysteries of an unknown tongue. The priest and the layman joined in the same immorality; they gamboled in the same licentious paths; nor did it cause a regret or raise a blush. The moral sense of the age was deadened, its religious one was gone. The night of error veiled the earth, and the plague of sin infected the people.

Against this despotism not a voice was lifted up, to stop this torrent of irreligion and sin not a hand was stretched out. Equal silence reigned in the schools of the learned as in the monasteries of the priest; universal submission prevailed among men; liberty wept over her degradation, truth mourned in her exile. Both despaired to return among men; when lo a voice was heard to break the silence; it was feeble, yet powerful; it was despised, yet it made the earth tremble. It was weak because it emanated from an obscure monk, it was strong because it was the voice of truth; it was contemned because the murmur of a humble ecclesiastic, it was feared because it was thought to be the trumpet of Heaven. It resounded from the walls of a monastery, its shrill yet solitary notes broke the sleep of men. Feeble at first, it strengthened; still and small in its beginning, it soon became sonorous and loud. Its teachings were first confined to a convent auditory; it speedily filled the earth and shook the foundation of the Pontiff's throne; it awoke mankind from the torpor of ages.

The voice was that of Luther. Goaded to the soul by the iron of slavery, his mighty spirit rebelled under the yoke. Stung by the abominations which surrounded him, his heart was incensed against the power which was their source. Nor was the fire thus kindled left to burn within the precincts of his own breast. The discontent which he felt within himself he communicated to others, the flame which kindled in his own breast was made to blaze for the illumination of the world. Nor did he shrink from a conflict with his antagonist; he dreaded not a contest with the foe. Strong in a conviction of the righteousness of his cause, he wavered not in his determination; covered with the armour of truth, he advanced boldly to the encounter. Nor was his fortitude long untested. Bulls from the Pontiff, sentences from councils, with slander and persecution from the multitude, deterred him not in his holy enterprise. His weapons of attack and defence were the tongue and pen. With these he had embarked in a contest with a power whose equal had not hitherto been seen in the world; with weapons apparently so feeble did he assail the massive citadel of Rome. Nor did he err in the choice of his arms, because often in the world's history has sword been conquered by the sword, but its voluminous pages record no instance of these weapons of the mind being overcome by so base an element. Never before or after did controversy excite such interest and emotion among men. Thermopylæ, Salamis, Philippi, Actium, Cressy, and Agincourt, are names which conjure up scenes that generated the deepest emotion of mankind, but the interest excited by the religious contest of the period under discussion probably exceeded the whole in intensity. And herein mankind judged rightly, because the results of the former but affected the freedom, the pride, the prowess or power of two contending nations, whereas those of the latter were intimately associated with the temporal and eternal well-being of the human race.

It was on these fields of public disputation, whereon were assembled monarchs and nobles, priests and people, that Luther had singly to maintain his cause. Unawed by the presence of royalty, the frowns of ecclesiastics, or the fury of the populace, the daring monk stood forth to vindicate freedom and truth. It was in this perilous arena that he had to demonstrate the soundness of his views. But his confidence was unbounded in the eventual triumph of truth over error, right over wrong. Nor was it misplaced; his appeals for truth met a response in the hearts of the people, his exposure of iniquity was hailed with satisfaction by men. The new doctrines gained ground; the converts were numbered by thousands. In the work of Reformation the pen followed the tongue, books succeeded sermons and harangues. Thus was the seed of truth sown, and at length it produced an abundant harvest. Daily was fresh impulse given to the movement, hourly did it grow in unity and strength. What shortly before was the delusion of an obscure monk, and at best a few followers, now became the received dogmas of the multitude and the cherished doctrines of crowned heads. The Reformer's firmness increased in proportion to the severity of the Pontiff's threats, his zeal grew in proportion to the persecution of his enemies. His was a great mind bent on a great object, and in its accomplishment his resolution never swerved. It was thus the foundation of the Pontiff's throne in Europe was shaken; thus the veil of error which for ages had covered the minds of men was rent, and the despotism of centuries was destroyed; thus was brought to pass that great event in the moral history of our race, the Reformation.

The blessings of the Reformation were not confined to the continental States which were the theatre of the insurrection, but England at the same time shared in the emancipation which was wrought. Although the Reformation in England ostensibly originated in the passions of the monarch rather than in the convictions of the people, still the same result followed as in the continental States where it emanated from purer sources, viz. the ejection of the papal sway. Still, neither in England nor elsewhere was it a complete emancipation of the church of Christ from unjust rule and unholy alliance. It was but a partial removal of the grievance which oppressed her; it was but a step, although a long one, towards the right goal. It liberated her only from the dominion of a spiritual despot, but left her still in alliance with the secular "powers that be." It but freed her from the double sword of the Pontiff, while she was joined in closer union with the sceptre of kings. It but released her from ecclesiastical tyranny, while she still heaved in unnatural connection with the principalities and powers of earth.

But a complete emancipation of the Christian

church from spiritual despotism and civil alliance was a measure not to have been expected from the first Reformers; it was an idea too large to have been originated by the same mind; the work was too stupendous to have been undertaken and perfected by the same agent. The discovery of truth has in all ages been gradual; its development and introduction into the habits, thoughts, and institutions of men have followed the same law. The entire of her arcana is not revealed at once, but like an Alpine valley its several parts are successively unfolded, view succeeds view with superadded lustre as the traveller advances on his course. Galileo discovered the earth's motion around the sun, and thus had a glance at the solar system; but a Newton must afterwards arise to harmonise the evolutions of the whole. A Bacon first pointed out the true road to knowledge; while a Kepler, a Davy, a Locke and a Reid must afterwards travel thereon and enrich the world with the treasures of the way. A Columbus first traversed the Atlantic and found a new continent beyond the blue of its deep, while a Drake must subsequently push farther the vessel's keel, and plough a Pacific whose ocean bed terminates but with the poles of the earth. Following the same law, it was enough for a Luther to have exposed the enormity of an ecclesiastical despotism and rescued mankind from its sway; while he left to others the discovery of the unholiness of the union which still remained between the church of Christ, the fair daughter of the skies, and the civil power, the corrupt man-child of earth.

The blaze of the Reformation was now over; its din, which filled Europe, had, like the last murmuring of the shore-stricken wave, died away on the ears of men; the volcano had exhausted its force; religious Europe had regained a calm. Peace and serenity appeared to fill its firmament. The *rôle* of ages progressed undisturbed by any grave collision or strife. It was supposed that the vessel of Christianity had now been moored into a safe harbour; that she had found a lasting resting place from the quicksands of error and the surges of popular thought. It was supposed that the church of Christ had at length been planted on a rock that would stand impregnable against the swell of human feeling and the tide of human opinion; it was supposed she had reached immutability. But this only furnishes another instance of the short-sightedness and fallibility of man, for erroneous was the supposition and vain the confidence, as the sequel of history proves.

In the middle of the sixteenth century there arose in England a spirit of dissatisfaction with the national Church, although reformed after the principles of Luther. Some minds cogitated on the new state of things, and thought that reformation was still needed, that a large portion of the leaven of Rome and of antichrist still lingered in the national Church. They first objected to the mode of worship adopted therein; they charged her with still preserving the relics of Romanism in the pomp of her forms and the gorgeousness of her ceremonies. They also charged her with a laxity of internal government and discipline. They wished to *purify* her still further from the errors and corruption of Rome, they pleaded for a *purer* mode of worship and discipline. Hence they were called Puritans. This name, though probably first intended as one of opprobrium, was happily given, and as truly characterized the men to whom it was applied. *They* were Puritans in every sense of the term—Puritans in religion, politics, and morals. Their conduct was holy, their principles pure, their sacrifices for conscience sake were great and astounding. They were the fathers of that mighty race of whom even Hume testifies: " So absolute indeed was the authority of the Crown, that the precious spark of liberty had been kindled, and was preserved, by the Puritans alone, and it was to this sect . . . that the English owe the whole freedom of their constitution." They were the founders of that section of Christians which so increased and decreased through the summers and winters of succeeding reigns, but during the last and present centuries have multiplied and filled the land. They were the generators of that spirit which through successive ages has preserved England from anarchy on the one hand, and misrule and despotism on the other. They were the impersonation of those great principles of freedom and truth which have made England so celebrated and the character of her people so renowned. Their conduct was magnanimous, their names are venerable, and their memories should be embalmed in every righteous breast. The very shades of those men rise up to rebuke their modern descendants; and when we measure ourselves with these champions of liberty, we feel our degeneracy, and blush for the contrast. Let the mantle of reverence enshroud their names, and let us press forward in their path and emulate their deeds.

But to return. Edward the Sixth ascended the throne of his ancestors in January, 1547, in the tenth year of his age. It is during the reign of this youthful monarch that we find the Puritans multiply and acquire strength as a body. Under the sunshine of this reign the pure principles of the Reformation flourished and spread; the precious plant thrived in a genial atmosphere. But this sunshine was of short duration, for this amiable prince was gathered to his fathers in the year 1553 after a reign of only seven years, a bud of great promise, snatched in springtime, ere its branches were fully unfolded or its graces shown. He was succeeded by his sister Mary, a name associated with all the horrors of persecution and martyrs' deaths. Thoroughly popish herself, she wished to mould her people into the same faith. She desired to re-establish the Pontiff's throne in England, and to re-enact the drama of papal tyranny and priestly sway. Nor did she lack the intolerance and cruelty which were necessary to carry her designs into execution. The Puritan reformers were numerous in the land. They offered a great stumbling-block to the accomplishment of the monarch's wishes, the re-establishment of the papal sway. They must be removed; argument would not do, for in this they were stronger than their enemies. Threats failed, because in their minds the menaces of an earthly monarch were drowned in the counter-threats of the King of heaven. There remained the prison, the scaffold, and the stake; and these were plied into the service. The prisons teemed with Puritan reformers, the scaffold reeked with their blood, and the stake blazed with their bodies.

The penal statutes passed in the reigns of Richard the Second, Henry the Fourth, and Henry the Fifth, against the Lollards or Protestants, were now revived and enforced with the utmost severity. The Queen, without the consent of her Parliament, appointed an ecclesiastical commission armed with all the enormous powers of the Inquisition in her husband's Catholic Spain, to punish heretics and extirpate heresy. The commission was composed of the most fierce and bloodthirsty Papists, presided over first by Bishop Gardiner, then Chancellor, (whose obdurate disposition was unequal to the sanguinary duties required from him, and he consequently retired,) and afterwards by the atrocious Bonner, Bishop of London, whose spirits were never so buoyant as when he tortured Protestants and massacred heretics by the express command of his august mistress the Queen.

The whole of this monarch's reign was dyed with the blood of martyrs; in the annals of history it is distinguished for nought but its cruelty. Had he not to record the sufferings and death of a Hooper, Latimer, and Ridley, with others their fellows, the historian would pass over this reign with a blank page. But it stands forth a foul leprosy on the leaves of British history. At length, after a reign of five years four months and eleven days, Mary died, terminating a reign of terror and a life of odium and misery. She then went to pass her account before the dread inquisition of Heaven.

The history of this reign abundantly demonstrates the inability of fire and sword to stop the progress of truth. For surely if ever moral truth could be extinguished by material elements, the problem would have been solved in this age. Never before or after was its smoking flax so beset with the showers of earthly persecution, hostility, and war; never was greater attempt made to uproot spiritual plant by carnal hands. But the attempt only served to fan the smoke into a flame, and to strengthen the roots of the plant. The Christian truths which the martyrs of Mary's reign carried with them into the flames came out like gold, the purer and more attractive in the eyes of men. They snatched brightness from the fire, their loveliness was developed by the blaze, their votaries therefore multiplied and grew. But the arrogance of man, by carnal weapons to attempt the destruction of truth! Does he know the Power with whom he contends? Is he aware that he has embarked in a conflict with Heaven, his Maker, his God? Does he know that he wages war with the eternal throne of the skies?

Elizabeth's accession to the throne was hailed by the nation and by the Puritan reformers. It was supposed that her Protestant character and profession augured well for the religious freedom of men. The Puritans therefore thought the winter of their sufferings was past, and a springtime had arrived.

But the thought proved vain, the expectation a dream! Elizabeth proved herself to be the transcript, the fit daughter, of Henry the Eighth. She thought she had a better right over the consciences than the persons of her subjects, that she had a diviner right to legislate for their religious belief than for the security of their property. She deemed it a more important and necessary duty to prescribe the religious creed of her people than to direct their conduct in the civil affairs of life. As the soul is more important than the body, she thought it her prior duty to legislate for the welfare of the first, and to cause it to think and act according to her own pet system of belief.

Acting upon these views, she caused to be passed, shortly after her accession, an Act the sole object and effect of which was to substitute Elizabeth for the Pope, to vest the English monarch with all the powers over and immunities in the Church, which the Pontiff once possessed. This statute annexed to the British Crown supremacy in ecclesiastical affairs, empowered the king or queen to repress all heresies, to establish or repeal any canons, to alter any point of discipline, and to ordain or abrogate any religious rite or ceremony. In the repression of heresy the monarch was only limited to the punishment of such doctrines as had been adjudged heresy on the authority of Scriptures by the first four general Councils, or by any general council which followed the Scripture as their rule, or of such other doctrines as should be thereafter denominated heresy by the Parliament and Convocation.

In the exercise of this power, the monarch was to be assisted by commissioners, either laymen or ecclesiastics, to be nominated by the Crown. The latter was the foundation of that tribunal infamous to posterity, the High Commission Court. Nor was this Act allowed to remain a dead letter on the pages of the statute book, nor did the High Commission Court slumber in inactive repose. By virtue of the powers which the former conferred, Elizabeth formed the religious belief, and directed the religious conduct of her people, with the same freedom and exactness as she would order her own household affairs. She prescribed laws for their thought and rules for their action. She addressed the mind in the profane language of the Danish chief: "Hitherto shalt thou go, and no farther." She drew the landmarks of thought on the frail pages of the statute book; she would have confined the eternal heavings of the soul within the feeble bounds of an act of parliament or government decree; she would have stopped truth in its everlasting career. But the eagle would not be bounded in his flight, nor the ocean cease its surge, although a monarch's voice pronounced the decree.

The High Commission Court was not designed to be a pleasant bauble or for empty parade. It was established to act, it was created to accomplish the monarch's ambition and wish. That ambition was to rule supremely over the minds as she already did over the property of her subjects; that wish was to subordinate their consciences to her absolute control. Nor did she lack fitting ministers to attempt the task; suitable dignitaries occupied the seats of the High Commission Court. They soon showed the nation that they held no sinecure office, that the power they wielded was not the mere pageantry of form. Wheresoever a book was to be found that did not accord with the established canon of law, the heretical volume was sought, its possessor seized and brought before the High Commission Court to answer for his crime. If a few Christians should assemble within unconsecrated walls to worship the God of their fathers in the purity and zeal of their hearts, the meeting was dispersed by the myrmidons of law, the assembled Christians apprehended and brought to answer for their offence before the same tribunal. Should any one, impressed with his allegiance to the King of Heaven, be heard to deny the supremacy of the British Queen, a grave offence was committed, and its author must abide the sentence of the High Commission Court. Many a Puritan hero paid for his religion with his life, many more for their conscience sake suffered the pains of imprisonment, exile and confiscation of goods. Thus was the precious spark of religious liberty attempted to be extinguished in our land; thus was the ever springing fountain of truth attempted to be dried up.

But it happens in the moral phenomena of this world that the means which are intended to produce a given result as frequently accomplish the opposite; that the means which are levelled for the destruction of truth as frequently contribute to its growth and accelerate its progress. Thus the arrow shot from the bow, failing in its mark, by a sort of just reaction recoils upon the archer, and wounds the hand that impelled its flight. This truth is fully demonstrated in the transactions of Elizabeth's reign; the persecutions were levelled at the extinction of puritanism in England, whereas they only increased its growth, and converted the smoking flax into—flame. The existing members of the body were the more rooted in their principles and confirmed in their faith by the hostility of rule and the rage of power. As the ivy clings to the oak with firmer grasp when the latter bends its head to the tempest, so did the Puritan of Elizabeth's reign hold his religion in closer embrace when the storm of persecution rolled over him and his faith. Common calamity is known to strengthen the bond of friendship; so was the Puritan the more wedded to his creed by the suffering he endured in its cause. Like the knight of chivalric days he only prized his fair one the more that he gained her by fight, and by the blood which in the conflict he shed.

Moreover, the persecutions of Elizabeth's reign but attracted the attention of mankind the more to the persecuted and their creed. The men who suffered were known for their purity and worth, and they evoked the sympathy of men. They were moreover known to be incomparably superior to their persecutors in every trait of human goodness, and thus fired the anger of men against their oppressors. From sympathy and esteem for the sufferers people desired to know why they suffered. They were therefore induced to examine their creed; they were led into investigation and inquiry, sure precursors of light and reformation; they compared the system with the Bible, and found it not inconsistent with the doctrines of that blessed Book. On the contrary, they found it more consonant with it than the vaunted dogmas of their unrighteous persecutors. Sympathy for the men was therefore exchanged for admiration of their creed; esteem for the persecuted was enlarged to love for the truth which they held. By this means an impulse was given to the Puritan movement, which the absence of persecution and state hostility might never have occasioned; yea, possibly greater than had it even basked in the sunshine of royal favour and grace.

During this reign puritanism, as it had been theretofore professed, was to undergo a change; it was to put on a still purer garment, a new phase was to be added to its character, it was to make a further retreat from the national Church. Theretofore puritanism only wished to make the national Church more pure in its doctrines and mode of worship. It did not wish to wean her from her ally, the State; it did not even complain that she enjoyed the support of the secular power. Its only complaint was that she did not employ the sceptre and sword to inculcate *pure* Christianity, that the civil power was not in alliance with the truth. It assumed, yea admitted, the legitimacy of the union; it would itself have entered the alliance. Its only complaint was that itself was not folded in the arm of civil power instead of its opponent, the national faith. This was therefore the point in dispute between puritanism on the one hand and the national establishment on the other. But others were now to be added, the breach was to become wider, the chasm deeper.

About the year 1580 arose one Robert Brown, who became the enunciator of new principles, the founder of a new sect in England. He was descended from an ancient family, and had been educated for the Church. Whether he was the first discoverer of the truths, or, which is more probable, had received them from others and was the mere enunciator of them in public, it is certain that about this time he began to promulgate principles of wider departure from the Established Church. He preached the doctrine of the entire and unmixed spirituality of the church of Christ. He therefore claimed its separation from the State. His doctrine was that the reigning monarch was only the head and governor of the civil community, and that his interference as such in the Christian church was an intrusion and an usurpation of the authority of Christ; that the earthly sovereign was head over his subjects civilly, but that Christ alone was Head of His church. He denied the right of the civil magistrate to interfere as such in declaring the truth in religious matters, or in compelling support or sanction to any system of religious belief. He also denied the right of the Crown to appoint spiritual rulers and pastors for the people, contending that such should be elected by the people themselves. He also maintained that each assembly or church of professing Christians should have their own government, and not be subject to any rule or authority of the civil power.

Brown for several years preached these doctrines with success, and made many converts to his creed. Driven by persecution he appears to have removed to Middleburgh in Zealand, where he formed a church after his own views. He afterwards returned to England, where he continued the propagation of his principles. During this time he suffered great persecution, having as he declared been confined in thirty-two prisons, in some of which he suffered much privation. Not being a very consistent character, Brown at length returned to the bosom of the Established Church, and died a very indifferent character in her communion. It is regretful that a life which commenced so auspiciously should have terminated so ingloriously, but Brown's history showed his want of that which alone could give strength and stability to his character, viz. love to God and a disinterested love of truth. Much of his conduct may be attributed to morbid ambition, a desire of popularity, fanatical zeal, or a spirit of party opposition.

But, though the man was frail and inconstant, the principles which he promulged were immortal; they survived; they could not die, because they were founded on eternal truth. The vessel is admitted to have been brittle and imperfect, but the water it contained was of crystalline purity; it therefore remained and flowed, after the vessel which had contained it was wrecked. Though the character of the sower was doubtful, he scattered good seed; it took ground, it germinated, it sprung. The principles which were once propagated, but afterwards forsaken, by Brown were imbibed by men of consistent character, disciples worthy of their faith.

Among these stand honourably the names of Barrow and Ainsworth. They continued the work which had been forsaken by Brown; they propelled the plough which he had ignominiously left; the purity of their morals, combined with the truth of their doctrines, gained them allies, they made many converts to their faith. Puritanism advanced with firm and rapid step; but its propagators were not unmolested, they were obliged to pay the penalty which the advocate of new truths in church or state has in all ages undergone, viz. the hostility and persecution of men. Many of these "excellent of the earth" were obliged to leave the land of their fathers and the home of their affections, and to seek refuge on a foreign shore, where they might worship their God after the dictates of their hearts; the country which cast its sheltering wing over these exiles for truth's sake (to its everlasting honour be it spoken) was Holland. There in those times the Puritan reformer found the home of freedom; there his prayer and thanksgiving ascended undisturbed to the God of his love.

The enemies of the new faith adopted two ways for its injury,—nicknaming and persecution. Aware that the character of Brown, its promulgator, was but indifferent, they thought no better means for its counteraction could be adopted than to associate the character of the man with his principles, and to call the latter after his name. The professors of the new faith were therefore called Brownists. By this means the enemy thought to translate the man into his creed, to affix indelibly the odium which covered the preacher, to his faith. There was in this conduct much policy, if no honesty; much knowledge of human nature, if no candour towards a foe. Few comparatively among mankind have, in more enlightened times than those of which we are speaking, been able to separate principles from their professors; to poise the former in the balance of truth without regard to the individuals who entertain them. Mankind have in all ages blended these two subjects; they have confused the man with the principles which he professed. If his character be imperfect, his creed is visited with a taint; if his conduct be exceptionable, his views are subjected to the same charge. It is thus that fresh truths, which are unpalatable to men, are by them identified with their disseminator whenever the character of the latter affords ground for accusation or charge. It was therefore policy in the enemies of nonconformity to call it by the name of Brownism and its professors Brownists. They thought this a likely means to condemn the new theology in the public mind, to brand it with disrepute in the estimation of men; and, doubtless, in many instances it had that effect. Brownism lost many an ally because of its name. But for this accidental and unhappy association, nonconformity would in all probability at this period have advanced with a bolder and more prosperous stride, and its success would have been greater. Everybody could not overstep the *man*, to his system; many stumbled in the attempt. Truth was therefore sacrificed at the shrine of the accidental in things.

The persecutions which were levelled at the extinction of nonconformity in this reign were various. Upon the death of Grindall, Archbishop of Canterbury, in the year 1583, Whitgift was appointed his successor in the archiepiscopal see. In the former the Puritans found a friend, or at least a favourable enemy; but the succession of the latter was to them a signal of persecution and strife. In Whitgift Elizabeth found a man after her own heart, a minister that would lend himself to all her purposes of ambition and power.

One of the first acts of Elizabeth after his elevation to the see was the reconstruction of the Court of Ecclesiastical Commission. The powers of the new court were more extensive than those of its predecessor, and its authority was more absolute. It consisted of forty-four commissioners, of whom twelve were ecclesiastics. Three commissioners formed a quorum. Hume, with all his bias to the throne and church, says of this tribunal: "The jurisdiction of this court extended over the whole kingdom and over all orders of men; and every circumstance of its authority, and all its methods of proceeding, were contrary to the clearest principles of law and natural equity. The commissioners were empowered to visit and reform all errors, heresies, schisms; in a word, to regulate all opinions, as well as to punish all breach of uniformity in the exercise of public worship. They were directed to make inquiry not only by the legal methods of juries and witnesses, but by all other means and ways which they could devise; that is, by the rack, by torture, by inquisition, by imprisonment. When they found reason to suspect any person, they might administer to him an oath called *ex-officio*, by which he was bound to answer all questions, and thereby might be obliged to accuse himself or his most intimate friend. The fines which they levied were discretionary, and often occasioned the total ruin of the offenders, contrary to the established laws of the kingdom. The imprisonment to which they condemned any delinquent was limited to no rule but their own pleasure. They assumed a power of imposing on the clergy any new articles of subscription, and consequently of faith, which they thought proper. Though all other spiritual courts were subject, since the Reformation, to inhibition from the supreme courts of law, the ecclesiastical commissioners were exempted from that legal jurisdiction, and were liable to no control. And, the more to enlarge their authority, they were empowered to punish all incests, adulteries, fornication, outrages, misbehaviours, and disorders in marriage; and the punishments which they might inflict were according to their wisdom, conscience, and discretion. In a word, the court was a real Inquisition, attended with all the iniquities, as well as cruelties, inseparable from that tribunal."

With powers so terrific was that court armed which was designed for the extirpation of puritanism in England. Nor did it remain dormant. Many were the culprits brought to answer at the bar of this monstrous tribunal. Extreme were the measures adopted to extort confession from, and otherwise to criminate, the innocent men. The jails were filled by its order; many an exile by its decree parted with the land of his fathers; and several illustrious reformers expiated their supposed guilt on the scaffold. Among the latter stand effulgently the names of Barrow, Greenwood, and Penry. These illustrious characters sealed their principles with their lives, and were lifted to the scaffold to be monuments for posterity of the purity of their faith and the ardour of their love to the God whom they adored. Such men stand on the shore of time like majestic rocks to stem the surges of human corruption and error. Long may they lift their proud crests to the skies, hurling terror to tyrants, and breaking the rage of the tempest to the wave-tossed mariner on the same stormy seas.

In the 35th year of Elizabeth's reign was passed an Act which fully demonstrates the persecuting character of the times. It was entitled "An Act to retain her Majesty's subjects in due obedience." Its penalties were directed against rebellious sectaries and disloyal persons. In this reign these two characters were always classed together; the conscientious dissenter from the established creed was identified with the rebel and insurgent. This statute enacted that any person above sixteen years of age, who obstinately refused during the space of a month to attend public worship in an established church, should be committed to prison. If, after having been committed for the offence, he should continue three months in his refusal, he must abjure the realm. Should he refuse this condition, or return after banishment, he should suffer capitally as a felon without benefit of clergy, which absurd phrase meant that his sentence should not be mitigated. Thus, in the Elizabethan age,—so eulogised for the richness of its literature, the depth of its science, and the extent of its political sagacity,—was passed an Act so subversive of right and revolting to reason; in an age so recent, and by the suffrages of the people's assembly, was enacted a measure so pregnant with the darkest iniquity, and which outraged all the instincts of human nature itself. Thus by an act of parliament did a tyrant queen and bigoted monarch attempt to fix the metes and bounds of human thought, by the feeble voice of a parliamentary statute did these empirics endeavour to suppress the spirit's immortal yearnings after truth. Wiser would it have been for Elizabeth and her parliament to have attempted by statute to remove the Andes, to dry the waters of the ocean, or to quench the volcano's flame.

Goaded by these persecutions, many a spirit looked abroad for the peace which it could not find at home; anguished by these measures many a heart panted for a shore where the tyrant's sway was unknown. To the persecuted Puritan of Elizabeth's reign Holland was the land of his love and the haven of his desire. There he found an ark of deliverance from the troubled waters of his mother land; on her shores waved serenely the olive branch of peace, over her sod hung unclouded freedom's fair sky. Thither, therefore, the persecuted Puritan hied.

Among others who sought refuge in Holland from the persecutions of their native land was John Robinson, a clergyman who had embraced the principles of the Brownists. He so far modified the principles of the new sect as to assimilate them more to modern Congregationalism. He is therefore generally regarded as the father of the Independents in England. This brave man and a band of faithful followers had, towards the close of Elizabeth's or the beginning of James's reign, reached the Dutch shores in safety. They settled in Leyden, and there formed a church. To this little band of expatriated people, — exiles for conscience sake,—did Robinson minister for a series of years. In their adopted country they could worship God after the dictates of their own heart, and highly did the little colony appreciate the blessing. But the genius of congregationalism was not suitable to the Dutch character. The small church at Leyden was, after a lapse of some years, found to diminish. The children of the exiles, by marriage and otherwise, merged into Dutch feeling and sentiment, and were gradually leaving the fold and faith of their fathers. Fearing therefore that the light which they had preserved at so much cost, and had introduced into Holland, and which they valued more than their lives, would not only wane but be extinguished if they remained in that country, many seriously cogitated emigration to the New World, there to plant a colony and establish their faith. At length, after many deliberations, a portion of the church at Leyden, in the year 1620, sailed for the shores of the new continent, and towards the close of that year they landed at New Plymouth. After many trials, privations, and hardships, the exiles founded a colony in that part of the new world theretofore called Virginia, but now known by the name of New England. There also they established their faith, and, finding a more congenial soil than in the Old World, it struck its roots deeply into the American mind, and now spreads its branches through the length and breadth of that flourishing land. Thus the seed, wind-blown by persecution, found a lodgment on the shores of the New World, and produced that great and prosperous nation which now bids fair to outlustre the richest kingdoms of the Old. The remainder of the church at Leyden continued under the care and ministry of Robinson until the latter was removed from his earthly labours by an ague on the 19th of February, 1624. Soon afterwards the remainder of the church followed their brethren to the shores of New England, and assisted in establishing their communion and perpetuating their faith. At length, under the fruitful labours of these devoted colonists, the deserts of America became a garden, and its wilderness blossomed like a rose. Happy for America was the arrival on its shores of the Pilgrim Fathers, auspicious the day when the fires of their encampment crackled in the solitude of its forests. They founded its greatness, they laid the pillars of its strength, they add, and will add, radiance to its present and future fame.

To sum up the character of this reign in its relation to nonconformity, it will have been seen that its most distinguishing trait was the spirit of persecution. Elizabeth herself was in sentiment more Romanist than Protestant. She assumed the latter only to exercise over the English Church the supremacy which the Pontiff enjoyed over that of Rome. She would not be a Catholic, because one of its conditions is spiritual obedience to the papal throne; this obedience Elizabeth exacted from others, rather than yielded it herself; she would contend with the Pope for spiritual dominion, and would wrest the sceptre from his hand; she would be pontiff over the Anglican Church. Her bigotry and intolerance were great, and gave a tone and character to her reign. None of the milder virtues flourished within her breast, and her spirit of persecution was strong. To the woe of mankind she found a servile ministry and obsequious parliament to accomplish her projects; the Puritan found her reign one continuous winter of persecution, more extensive, though not so unblushingly cruel as that of her sister and predecessor, Mary. It had acquired a milder form and more specious appearance than the latter; but by reason of this quality it was perpetrated on a wider scale. The forms of legal procedure were not so openly renounced, nor the gradation of supposed offences so wantonly outraged as in Mary's reign; yet the victims of persecution were more numerous, and the sum total of their sufferings greater. It does not appear that in this reign whosoever had any book on heresy, treason or sedition, "and should not presently burn them without reading them or showing them to any other person, should be esteemed a rebel and without any further delay be executed by martial law"; yet the same enormities were perpetrated under a more specious guise. The High Commission Court gave a plausibility to the proceeding, and a pretext for the condemnation; yet its power was for this reason only the more dangerous, and the exercise of it more severe. In short, the modern nonconformist may justly regard the reign of Elizabeth as a fit continuation of that of Mary, and both may descend to ignominious immortality in the same ecclesiastical category.

Notwithstanding these persecutions, puritanism and nonconformity increased rapidly in England during the reign of Elizabeth; though cradled in the storm, like the eagle, like him they grew and strengthened in its midst. Nonconformity was much stronger at the close of Elizabeth's reign than at her accession, its votaries were more numerous, and had deeper insight into the principles of their faith. They had been taught firmness by persecution, they had acquired learning by controversy. Their views of religion were clearer than those of their forefathers; their conviction of the truth of their creed better founded and more stable. Their houses of meeting were greatly multiplied, the congregations which frequented them had enlarged, and the sect was dignified by the membership of some senators of the land. Puritanism was before strong; it was now invincible, it had raised its head above the waters and would be no longer submerged. Monarchs feared and trembled because they saw a power arise which would furnish an everlasting barrier against tyranny and wrong. The friends of liberty hailed it as a messenger of good, its steady success brightened the career of truth. But this was only the beginning of its achievements, the dayspring of its light, the dawning of its glory.

Elizabeth departed to her fathers on the 24th of March, 1603, in the forty-fifth year of her reign, and was succeeded by James, king of Scotland. The nonconformists of this period comprised the Presbyterian, Independent, and Baptist denominations. They rejoiced at the accession of James to the throne of England, for, knowing that he had been educated in the Presbyterian principles of Scotland, they hoped for favour and toleration from him, and a relaxation of the rigorous laws which were passed in the previous reigns against nonconformity. Accordingly, on his entrance into England to assume the British crown and sceptre, he was met on the way by a deputation of the puritan or nonconformist party, who presented him with a petition called the millenary, embodying the wishes of a thousand ministers for further reformation in religion. It expressed a hope that James, having received his education in Scotland, and having some time professed his attachment to its established church, would at least abate the rigour of the laws which in previous reigns had been enacted against nonconformity, if he did not go further and show the Puritans favour. But they had soon reason to know that they had greatly erred in their opinion respecting the protestantism of James and the liberality of his religious sentiments. They soon found that his private creed was nearer allied to popery than protestantism; and instead of the religious tolerator whom they vainly pictured him to be, they had a meddling bigot and ruthless despot. Instead of uprightness of conduct, they found in the new prince the greatest deceit and vacillation, and instead of sanctity of manners they met with nought but profligacy, dissipation, and vice. Nor did he long conceal his hostility to the Puritans, it was early discovered in the measures which he pursued. This prince presents the picture of a weak monarch attempting to check the aspirations of a people who were great and determined to be still greater, of an imbecile sovereign sitting at the head of a nation teeming with liberal and patriotic designs.

In the year next after his accession we find James summoning a conference between the High Church and Puritan parties, to be held at Hampton Court. James, presuming upon great depth of theological learning, intended to act as arbitrator between the contending parties and to make the occasion a theatre for the display of his lore. The disputants on both sides were nominated by the King with the advice of his Privy Council. On the Church side were eight bishops and eight deans; for the Puritans there were but four. At the head of the assembly the vain King sat, aided by his Privy Council. The subjects discussed at this conference do not appear to have been of vital importance, and according to Mr. Hume they were the cross in baptism, the ring in marriage, the use of the surplice, and the bowing at the name of Jesus. But probably graver and more momentous questions were introduced into the discussion, if not in the list appointed for the occasion. The tenour and result of this meeting is differently represented by writers according to their partiality to the one or other of the contending parties. But it may be assumed as a fact that the King and his ministers thoroughly sided with the Church party, and that by the whole of them the Puritan advocates were rudely and unceremoniously treated. The result was what might have been anticipated from such an assembly; the contending parties separated with mutual dissatisfaction, and the breach between them widened by the affray. The only good effects were a few amendments of the liturgy, and the appointment of a committee of divines to translate the Bible into the English language; the translation which emanated from this body is the one at present in general use. Thus the professed object of the conference, the settlement of the differences between the Church party and the Puritans, was frustrated, while the collateral advantages we have named emanated from its discussions.

The spirit of persecution prevailed to a very considerable extent in this reign, although much mitigated since the times of Mary and Elizabeth.

This was probably not owing so much to any more tolerant disposition on the part of James as to the more advanced public opinion of the people. The King would in all probability have enforced the powers of the High Commission Court against the Puritans as vigorously as any of his predecessors, if he could have done so with the same impunity from the public mind. James was inwardly not the less a tyrant and persecutor than Mary and Elizabeth, but his natural disposition was concealed and restrained by the opinion of his subjects. Thus in most ages the tyrant has in his career of despotism met with salutary check and resistance from the public opinion of the people; this appears to be the sea bank raised by Providence against the extravagant swell of human tyranny, the natural barrier to its desolating advance. To this cause was owing the absence in this reign of those scenes of persecution and bloodshed which so defile the reigns of Mary and Elizabeth on the historian's page. The laws against puritanism under which the iniquities of the former reigns were perpetrated were still in force, and wanted but the favourable voice of the people to burst their bonds and desolate England with their malignity. The High Commission Court still existed, but its arms were fettered and its spirit checked by the salutary opinion of the age. By this means tyranny was compelled to hold its revels in moderation, while liberty was allowed to lift its head above the waters of persecution and strife.

The greatest foe and persecutor of the Puritans in this reign was Bancroft, Archbishop of Canterbury. He pursued this body with all the malignant hostility and persecution which the spirit of the age would allow. It appears that in one year of his ecclesiastical ascendancy three hundred ministers were suspended, deprived, excommunicated, imprisoned, or forced to leave their country by reason of their holding or being suspected to hold puritan opinions. He was a fit successor of Whitgift in the Canterbury see, and would have acquitted himself well at the head of a Spanish inquisition. But fortunately the public opinion of the times furnished a barrier to his violence and rage. He was succeeded in his functions by Archbishop Abbot, whose leniency to the Puritans and general attachment to liberty offered a pleasing contrast to his predecessor's character and life. During the archiepiscopacy of Abbot puritanism advanced more boldly and multiplied the converts to its faith; the general intolerance of the Canterbury see was even at this period sometimes relieved by a gleam of prelatical mildness and liberality, as the darkest night is occasionally brightened by the appearance of an auspicious star.

This reign furnishes several instances of extremest persecution for holding religious tenets unauthorised by law. Two Arians were for their opinions consigned to the flames. A third would have followed, but that a revolt of public opinion stayed the execution of the decree. Thus was developed the power which throughout James's reign stemmed the torrent of persecution and kept it within more moderate bounds. Wisely hath the Almighty implanted the instinct of humanity and justice so deeply in man.

Upon the whole, the measures of James's reign were not so hostile to puritanism as many of its friends had feared, and consequently its progress was steady and its success considerable. Under the partial torpor of the laws which in previous reigns had been enacted for its extinction, puritanism advanced and flourished. As the shrub lifts its head the more firmly once there is a cessation of the gale, the Puritans began to be favourably regarded by the men of power and estate in the country, and many of the persecuted members found shelter and a home beneath their roofs. The principles of the sect began to be more known, and therefore less feared and more beloved. The conduct of the Puritans themselves was more scrutinised, their worth was seen and admired. It was discovered that their principles were not dangerous, that the men who professed them were not disloyal, but that both were entitled to the respect and esteem of mankind. The principles therefore advanced, and their professors multiplied. At length James departed this life on the 27th of March, 1625, after a reign of twenty-two years and some days, leaving to posterity a character in which there is little to admire or imitate.

The sceptre of James descended to his son and successor, Charles, whose accession to the throne met with popular applause. The Puritans expected grace and favour from his hands, because they supposed him to have been partial to their party. This supposition was founded on the fact of his having been accompanied to London on his accession by Dr. Preston, the head of the Puritans; but their anticipations were doomed to disappointment equally with those of their predecessors in James's reign, for the new King soon proved himself to be the bigoted ally of episcopacy, if not the abettor of popery itself, and the intolerant foe of Puritan piety and faith. To the former he clung with all the devotion and pertinacity of fanatical zeal, while the latter he regarded as inimical to his interests and throne, and its professors he held in abhorrence as direct foes. Although Charles was doubtless naturally inclined to the love of episcopacy, with its gradation of orders and gorgeousness of rites, yet the feeling was much increased and the attachment strengthened by the influence of his primate, Laud. Happy in all probability would it have been for Charles if this ambitious individual had ever remained in the walks of ecclesiastical obscurity, and had never reached the elevated dignity of the Canterbury see, because it is certain that his intolerant spirit and persecuting administration much accelerated, if it did not materially cause, the fatal disasters which subsequently befell the unfortunate King. Charles, by his marriage with Henrietta, daughter of the king of France, a Romanist, was probably induced to look with a favourable eye on popery, if he did not entertain an inward desire for its communion. This feeling of the King was strengthened by the undisguised popish tendencies of Laud. The latter wanted nothing but profession to become completely Romanist. His alteration of the Church service, his exposition of her doctrines, and his innovations in her ceremonies, all tended directly to Romanism. The Church of England was in fact, shortly before the subversion of Laud's power, become popish in all but name, and in this the King cordially joined his primate. Even a project was at this time entertained of a union with Rome, and an emissary of the Pope was received by the King privately at court. Part of the council proposed and urged the union.

The popish emissary, Panzani, was assured by the Bishop of Chichester that the two archbishops, Canterbury and York, were willing to submit to the Pope, that there were only three of the English prelates adverse to the union, that the only difficulty in his own way was the doctrine of transubstantiation, and that a conference of moderate men on both sides would probably accomplish the desired union. The project failed simply by reason of the uncompromising spirit of Rome.

In proportion as he loved Rome did Laud abhor puritanism. If his love to the former was extreme, his hatred of the latter was equal. Its doctrines he denounced, its professors he reviled and punished. Enjoying the entire confidence of the King, and having power over those engines of despotism, the High Commission Court and Star Chamber, he readily plied the latter in his crusade against the Puritans, his foes.

Among those who suffered indignity and punishment from these infamous tribunals stand conspicuously the names of Burton, Prynne, and Bastwick. The first was a divine, the next a lawyer, and the last a physician. They had before been imprisoned for alleged libels, they were now accused of publishing fresh reflections on the bishops. After the most infamous trial, they were condemned to stand in the pillory and have their ears cut off, which sentence was accordingly executed. Even Dr. Leighton, one of the Church ministers and father of the celebrated archbishop, received a similar or worse sentence for lifting his voice against the popish abominations of the Church in a work entitled "An Appeal to the Parliament; or, Zion's Plea against Prelacy." The historian records that his ears were cut off, his nose slit, his face branded with burning irons; he was tied to a post and whipped with a triple cord, of which every lash brought away the flesh. He was kept in the pillory near two hours in frost and snow. He was afterwards imprisoned with great severity for about eleven years, and when eventually released he could not hear, see, or walk. Innumerable besides were the victims to Laud's cruel intolerance and rage.

Persecuted so severely at home, many of the Puritans looked towards other lands. Sick of the tyranny of the Old World, their eyes darted across the Atlantic to the New. There they saw a land, broad, fertile, and free, whose shores were untouched by persecution, and whose skies were unclouded by the fury of prelatical zeal. They saw that its broad expanse was unruffled by the oppression of home, they saw in it a refuge from present calamity, an asylum from years of suffering and wrong. Probably also they recollected the emigration thither of their persecuted brethren of Elizabeth's reign, and desired to follow in their wake. They pictured to themselves a colony of free-hearted men transported from scenes of oppression and sorrow to the quiet repose of an American plain, each labouring for the common weal, and all worshipping the God of their fathers according to the dictates and love of their hearts. This was their desire, this they saw awaiting them on New England's shores. And what though the broad Atlantic rolled between them and the land of their love? Were not the treasures of the country worth crossing the deep? Was not freedom—precious gem—worth traversing an ocean's breast? Would the Puritan's heart, that never quailed beneath the hurricane of persecution at home, tremble at the surge of a friendly sea? Would it not even be better to lie buried in the channels of an unconscious deep, with the rippling wave to sing a requiem over head, than to live and die in the land of the oppressor and foe?

It appears that during twelve years of Laud's administration no fewer than four thousand Puritans emigrated to America, and that about seventy-seven divines of the Church of England became pastors of emigrant churches in that country before the year 1640. These emigrants were not entirely composed of the poor, but included many who were both wealthy and considerable in the mother country. This emigration greatly impoverished the state by the loss of so much labour and wealth. It is computed that the emigration of this period drained England of half a million sterling, an immense sum in those days. The King, assisted by Laud, fearing the consequences of so extensive an emigration, and probably desirous of repressing puritanism throughout the world, resolved to prohibit the system. By an order in council, dated 6th April, 1638, all owners and masters of vessels were restrained from sailing with passengers to America without special licence. The effect of this order was to prevent eight ships loaded with Puritan emigrants, and then lying in the Thames, from proceeding to the colony of New England. Among other emigrants were persons of no less distinction than John Hampden, John Pym, Oliver Cromwell, and Sir Arthur Hazelrig. These zealous and patriotic men had determined to leave their native land, which they regarded as the Egypt of bondage, for a home of liberty in the New World. They had actually embarked on their voyage thither when the order in council was passed, which stopped them. An air of fatality appears to surround this transaction, when it is considered that the King by this very measure restrained within his dominion the men who at no very distant period caused the subversion of his power, and wrested the sceptre from his hand, and one of whom was destined to sit in his place on the British throne. Often does tyranny by its excesses nurture the seed of its own dissolution, as does the shrub the worm which will lay it low.

Charles's conduct in the civil affairs of his kingdom was the counterpart of that which he exercised towards religion. Athough he had a parliament he was determined to rule without them; as they were not completely obsequious to his will, he resolved to concentrate in himself the whole power of the state. He would enter into war without their knowledge, would levy taxes without their consent, and would negotiate treaties without their sanction. If any patriot raised his voice against the tyranny, he was lodged in the Tower as a rebel and traitor. His council consisted of a few unprincipled courtiers, his parliament of a low cabal. In all this Charles mistook the genius of his times, for this was changed since the reigns of the eighth Henry and Mary. There was a spirit of inquiry and freethinking abroad, of whose extent Charles was ignorant. There was also a spirit of resistance in his realm, of whose magnitude and power he never dreamt. This spirit was the offspring of the Reformation, and had been generated among the tumults and throes of those momentous times. It had in floating through the intervening ages acquired strength, and was now ripe for action. This spirit first awoke in the cloisters of religion, and afterwards visited the halls of state; it now filled the hemispheres of both. This spirit could ill brook the tyrannies and excesses of Charles, it could ill endure the rapacity and cruelty of Laud. It found suitable exponents in a Pym, a Hampden, a Cromwell, and a Vane. After many friendly warnings it came into collision with royal power and sacerdotal will. A struggle ensued, battles were fought, the contest was fierce and long continued, and success various, alternately crowning the banners of each; but at last the spirit of the age triumphed, and laid prostrate at its feet the demons of civil tyranny and religious wrong.

Among the crowning exploits of this memorable war was the destruction of those infamous tribunals, the High Commission Court and Star Chamber. These courts, after having been for ages the scourge of the country and the destroyers of its liberty, were abolished by the long parliament. Their iniquities were thenceforth to be found in history alone. Laud was impeached, committed to the Tower, and finally executed on the public scaffold. State episcopacy was abolished, and full toleration granted to all sects and parties. The sceptre was taken from Charles and wielded by the parliament. Monarchy was gone, and the parliament alone was omnipotent and supreme. In short, a complete transformation in the constitution and government of both Church and State followed this memorable struggle, and all in favour of the liberty, civil and religious, of the subject.

The two sects which were at this time most prevalent among the insurgent or parliamentary party were the Presbyterians and Independents. The most considerable men of the former were the Earls of Essex and Northumberland, Warwick and Denbigh, Sir Philip Stapleton, Sir William Waller, Hollies, Massey, Whitelocke, Maynard and Glyn; and of the latter were Sir Harry Vane, Oliver Cromwell, Nathaniel Finnis, and Oliver St. John, the solicitor-general. The triumph of the parliament having caused the abolition of State episcopacy and the deposition of Charles, a vacancy was opened for a religious ally to the reigning power. The Presbyterians, who were strongest in parliament, favoured by the assistance which the Scottish army rendered in the war against the King, secured the alliance. Presbyterianism therefore succeeded to episcopacy as the religion of the State. The former now became the parliamentary ally. In the exercise of power she did not appear to have profited much by the persecution she herself had endured during the ascendancy of the episcopal faith. On the contrary, she appears to have forgot all experience of the past, and to have plunged immediately on her elevation into all the bigotry and intolerance of prelacy, the previous ally. She would have passed laws to prevent heresy and schism, and would have punished their infraction with all the rigour of intolerant zeal. But fortunately the Independents (who were not inconsiderable in parliament, and strong in the country), assisted by Selden, Whitelocke, and other friends of religious freedom in the senate, frustrated the attempt of the Presbyterians to re-enact intolerant laws and to kindle anew the flames of religious persecution in the realm. The stronghold of presbyterianism was the parliament; that of independency was the army. During the ascendancy of the parliament the former enjoyed the distinction of being the religion of the State; but the conquest of the parliament by Cromwell and the army precipitated the downfall of its presbyterian ally. The sun which before shone on the Presbyterians now beamed on the Independents, and henceforth during the Commonwealth era independency enjoyed the favour of State. Now it was that the fullest toleration was enjoyed by all religious parties, because a distinctive feature of independency was freedom of thought and action, to all, in matters of religion and conscience; the Presbyterian and Episcopalian enjoyed the same right and liberty of worship as did the Independent, the favourite of the ruling power.

The conduct of the Independents in this particular contrasted advantageously with that of their predecessors the Presbyterians, when in the enjoyment of the same power. But the genius of the two systems was different, and sufficed to account for the opposite results. That of presbyterianism courted junction with the State, and would have used the sceptre and sword of the ally to enforce its discipline and advance its creed; that of independency shrunk from the union, and would have revolted from employing the civil power to propagate its faith. These different tendencies of the two prevailing religions are fully borne out by the prejudiced pen of Hume. He says: "The Catholics, pretending to an infallible guide, had justified upon that principle their doctrine and practice of persecution. The Presbyterians, imagining that such clear and certain tenets as they themselves adopted could be rejected only from a criminal and pertinacious obstinacy, had hitherto gratified to the full their bigoted zeal in a like doctrine and practice. The Independents, from the extremity of the same zeal, were led into the milder principles of toleration. . . . Of all Christian sects, this (the Independents) was the first which, during its prosperity as well as its adversity, always adopted the principles of toleration."

During the Commonwealth era the ranks of nonconformity were increased by the Quakers, or the Society of Friends. This sect, which afterwards considerably increased, and whose adhesion to their principles and sacrifices for their preservation have rendered them so celebrated, was founded by one George Fox, who was born at Drayton in Leicestershire, in the year 1624. After an eccentric youth, Fox commenced public preaching in the year 1647. The leading feature of the system which he promulged was the necessity for mankind receiving and improving the inward teachings of the Holy Spirit. Fox began to expound his principles in the parish churches, where he interrupted the ministers and disturbed the service. He was for a molestation of this sort imprisoned at Nottingham in 1649, and at Derby in 1650. Nothing dismayed by these and similar sufferings, Fox continued to expound his doctrines in the places of most public resort. At length, finding indoor worship more convenient, the Friends in the year 1654 hired the "Bull and Mouth" in Saint Martin's-le-Grand, London, for their services. The first ministers who officiated in this meeting-house were Francis Howgill and Edward Borough. The Friends still continued field and street preaching; their principles were well received in Bristol, where a prosperous society was founded. The progress of this sect awoke the apprehensions of Cromwell, and he required Fox not to disturb the Protector's government. Fox replied: "I do deny the wearing or drawing of a sword, or any outward weapon, against thee or any man."

This sect enjoyed a considerable share of toleration during the Commonwealth, and the zealous advocacy of its principles by Fox and his brethren multiplied its adherents and advanced its creed.

At length Cromwell departed this life on the 3rd of September, 1658. His character has been the subject of much comment and discussion by all the historians of the Commonwealth age. Perhaps no character in history has been the subject of a greater variety of opinions; and generally, each writer and class of writers indulging in praise or blame, according to the agreement or disagreement of Cromwell's principles with their views, the portraiture is comely or deformed just as it is drawn by a friendly or unfriendly hand. In the description of no public character has the writer's pen been more largely dipped in the honey or gall of personal feeling. By the Royalist he is accused of most of the crimes which can defile the citizen or the sovereign; whereas it is evident, from the current of history, that the Protector's virtues on these scores far outweighed his alleged defects. By the Episcopalian he is branded with intolerance, while the Presbyterian reverses the charge and accuses the Protector of excessive toleration of religious sects. That many parts of the Protector's character as a citizen and ruler are exceptionable must be admitted; but it is clear they did not outweigh or even equal his great merits. It must also be recollected, in forming an estimate of the Protector's character, that he was an extraordinary personage in extraordinary times; that many or perhaps most of his crimes were necessitated by the political condition of things; and that had his pathway been freer from this necessity, his conduct would have presented less guilt and fewer stains. That he granted religious toleration to an extent before and afterwards for ages unequalled is indisputable. That he favoured the Independents is allowed; and it is certain he was not guilty of a system of general persecution or even intolerance to any religious sect. The occasional outbursts of his administration in this way, particularly towards the Episcopalians, are attributable more to political necessity than to wanton guilt. This party was supposed to be continually plotting against his person and government, and it was to prevent or suppress these machinations that his occasional violence was designed. That the general tenor of his government embraced the principle of toleration is evident from the concurrent voices of all its historians; and this quality of his administration, for which he was so unsparingly reviled in his own times, is the surest basis of the Protector's present and future fame.

From the foregoing it may be inferred that

puritanism flourished in England during the Commonwealth era. Freed from the restraints of unjust laws and oppressive tribunals, its prosperity was rapid and great. The days of its bondage were gone, and the hour of its liberty and triumph was come. They came together; the day of her liberty was the day of her success. In the preceding ages she was feeble, because, like the bulrush, her head was continually exposed to the storm; but now that the calm had arrived she towered like a cedar, and spread her fostering branches through the land. Her awestruck and persecuting enemy, episcopacy, was no longer the religion of the State, but had changed places with her foe. The latter, after ages of undisputed supremacy, was at last hurled from the throne, and now wallowed in the dust. Her sting was taken away, though the venom might have remained. She was among the tolerated religions of the country. She was no longer the handmaid of the State, and the ally of civil authority; yet she was not in bondage, nor under restraint; she enjoyed liberty, full, free, and as much as she needed. The weapons of persecution alone were taken from her; her spiritual armour was left undisturbed, and this she had full freedom to ply. In this her victorious opponent displayed a magnanimity and forbearance which we seek in her own annals in vain. Ascendant puritanism cast aside her predecessor's persecuting lash. In the ordinary creed of men, it would have been but just retaliation if puritanism had inflicted on episcopacy the scourge which, in her more auspicious days, the latter had inflicted on the former. It would have been but trying her by her own code, and punishing her by her own law; complaint would therefore be excluded. But this puritanism forbore. She enriched the garland of conquest with the olive spray of mercy and peace; she pointed out to every future conqueror the way to enhance the honours of success.

In glancing at the Commonwealth era, the first thing that strikes the observer is the greatness with which the whole is surrounded; the greatness of the drama, and the equal greatness of the actors. The chief agents in accomplishing the great change were Puritans. It was puritanism which urged them to the encounter; it was for her they drew the sabre and unsheathed the sword. She was the queen whose cause they supported, and whose flag they unfurled. It was her spirit that made them heroic, it was for her they achieved the victory; the diadem was therefore placed on her brow.

The religious character of this period has been the subject of much difference of opinion and conflicting remarks. Some charge it with an exuberance of fanaticism and hypocrisy, while others laud it as the perfection of religious purity and zeal. Both descriptions are probably incorrect, and the mean of both would be near the truth; that there was much enthusiasm among the leading characters of this period is certain, and that they were candid there is every reason to conclude. To acknowledge that they are chargeable with enthusiasm is only to admit that human nature is prone to be extreme in its attachment to the idol of its love. Had the leaders of the change been less enthusiastic, they would in all probability never have consummated the great events of their age; had they been free from it altogether, they would probably never have hazarded the attempt, and England would have lost one of the brightest pages in its history.

Great as was this age in worldly enterprise and secular learning, it was also profound in its theological lore. Some of the ablest divines that England ever produced grace this period. Among them may be named Dr. John Owen, the prince of theologians, and Dr. Thomas Goodwin, scarcely his inferior in talents and learning; Thankful Owen, Porter, Charnock, Samuel Lee, Ralph Button, Jonathan Godard, Theophilus Gale, Thomas Cole (the tutor of the celebrated John Locke), and John Howe; all of whom belonged to the Independent party. The Presbyterians were honoured with the talents and learning of Drs. Wilkinson, Greenwood, Staunton, Conant, Harris, and Harman. The Episcopalians numbered the following distinguished men in their communion: Drs. Wilkins, Ward, Wallis, Pocock, Hugh, Hyde, and Bishop Barlowe. The foregoing is a galaxy of names that would render illustrious the religious character of any country or age.

Cromwell's sceptre was speedily wrested from his son and successor Richard, and was placed in the hands of Charles the Second. This period is called the Restoration. That rigid purity of morals which characterized the court during the Commonwealth era now gave way to immorality and licentiousness; that zeal for religion bordering on enthusiasm, which then prevailed in the higher circles of society, was displaced by infidelity or indifference. The Bible was no longer the treasure of the palace, morality ceased to be the study and practice of the court. The precepts of the holy Scriptures were openly contemned and violated by the King and his courtiers. Whereas, before, all the rites and ordinances of religion were scrupulously observed in the court and camp, now all manner of irreligion unblushingly prevailed. Then the practice of an austere morality was general among the higher classes of society, now it had abandoned their haunts. In thus bursting the restraints of religion and the bonds of morality, the King took the lead

F

of his subjects. Steeped in immorality, he blushed not at the stain; wallowing in licentiousness, he made no effort to conceal the mire. Royal example was potent with the multitude, who followed his steps; and this reign was deeply laden with guilt.

Charles's restoration to the throne appears to have been founded on his declaration of Breda, whereby he guaranteed full toleration of religion. How the King fulfilled his declaration the sequel will show. Shortly after Charles's accession the Act of Uniformity was passed. It required every clergyman to be reordained if he had not before received episcopal ordination, to declare his assent to everything contained in the Book of Common Prayer, to take the oath of canonical obedience, to abjure the solemn league and covenant, and to renounce the principle of taking arms on any pretence whatsoever against the King. By this act of enormous injustice Charles violated all his promises of toleration contained in the declaration of Breda. The most positive assurance, on which his restoration to the throne was mainly founded, was by this Act openly outraged. Thus was revived that legislation, so frequent in the reigns of Elizabeth and Mary, which attempted to coerce the conscience of man and control his belief. Now reappeared that spirit of opposition to free inquiry and that disposition to dictate creeds which was the ruling passion of the ancestors of Charles, but which had been buried in the ashes of the volcano that culminated in the establishment of the Commonwealth. But there were minds in this reign that would not even outwardly obey so monstrous a law. On St. Bartholomew's day, 24th of August, 1662, when the clergy were obliged to conform to this Act or relinquish their livings, two thousand clergymen obeyed the voice of conscience rather than that of the British parliament. They resigned their livings, and chose rather to endure poverty and privation than to sacrifice conscience on the altar of royal bounty and temporal emolument. It appeared that Bartholomew's day was artfully chosen by the enemies of freedom at this period, that the nonconforming clergy might lose their year's income, which would become due shortly afterwards. On the previous occasion, when on the ascendancy of the parliament the established clergy were deprived of their livings, one fifth of their former stipends was reserved for the support of the ejected ministers; but this act of charity was not repeated by Charles and his senate. Yet these were men equal to the emergency. They needed not temporal emolument to sustain their principle or fire their zeal. They derived their strength and succour from higher sources than parochial revenues. In their deepest distress they were fed by manna from above; during their darkest calamity they were enlivened by a heavenly ray.

Now the name of Puritan was exchanged for that of Nonconformist. In its ranks were included Presbyterians, Independents, Baptists, and Quakers. Although a storm threatened, and its first outburst had already descended upon them, the Nonconformists at this period were numerous and on the increase. The Act of Uniformity had added to their number and strengthened their cause. A measure so iniquitous was pregnant with benefit, because it separated the wheat from the chaff; it collected and united the friends of truth, who coalesced the more when they saw a common danger before them, and prepared to resist further attack. The Nonconformists of this period petitioned the King for an indulgence which, to shield the Roman Catholics (to whom he was inwardly much inclined) as well, he appeared disposed to grant; but the unwillingness of parliament frustrated the design. This parliament was not that of Cromwell, Vane and Essex, but an assembly of bigots in religion and empirics in politics, under whose feeble guidance England sunk into degradation and obscurity.

The measure of Charles's injustice was not yet complete. In 1665 an Act was passed that no dissenting teacher, who took not the oath of passive obedience and non-resistance, should, except upon the road, come within five miles of any corporation, or of any place where he had preached after the Act of Oblivion, under a penalty of £50 and six months' imprisonment. The object of this Act was to harass the Nonconformists the more by depriving their ministers of the means of procuring a livelihood. A blank still remained in the catalogue of Charles's persecutions, but this was filled by the Conventicle Act of 1670, which enacted that if any person above the age of sixteen years were present at any conventicle or place of worship different from the Church of England, where there should be more than five persons besides the household, he should for the first offence suffer three months' imprisonment or pay a fine of £5, for the second offence the punishment was doubled, and for the third the person offending should be banished to America or pay £100, and if he returned from banishment should suffer death. A clause was added that if in the interpretation of the Act any doubt should arise, the same should be explained by the judges in the sense least favourable to the conventicle, it being the intention of parliament entirely to suppress them. This clause outraged the first maxim of the criminal jurisprudence of England, viz. that the accused shall have the benefit of every doubt. But the senate that could be guilty of so great an enormity as to prevent the assembly of conscientious men for the worship of God could without scruple perpetrate the lesser one of declaring that the construction of the Act should be in the sense least favourable to the accused. By this time Charles and his parliament appear to have glutted their appetite for persecution. Nonconformity, like the galley slave, laboured in chains, while her rival travelled in the royal road of state favour and patronage.

The effect of these measures, and particularly of the Conventicle Act, was to fill the jails with victims, martyrs to religious truth. Many holy men were dragged from the temples of their God to the magistrate, and thence without ceremony to the prison, and there kept in bonds to expiate the guilt of worshipping God according to the dictates of their Bible and heart. The King, having at length taken umbrage at the conduct of some of the bishops and conforming clergy, meditated a scheme for toleration; but the fury of the religious controversy which arose at this period frustrated the design. The Act against conventicles was renewed with additional severity because now the protection of trial by jury, that palladium of English liberty, was taken from the accused, whose conviction might be founded on the oath of a single informer, who was rewarded by a third of the fine, an unrighteous reward of treachery and guilt. During all this time Charles had a great leaning for popery, if he were not actually far advanced in the way to her communion; and to favour the Papists, who were equally with Nonconformists obnoxious to the persecuting laws, he published a declaration for indulgence and suspending all penal laws against Dissenters, and authorising them to meet in places of worship licensed by the King. Henceforth during this reign the Nonconformists enjoyed greater freedom of worship. Had not Charles felt an affection for Rome, the nonconformist fetters would have remained unbroken, and the close of this monarch's reign would have been stained with the cruel persecutions which characterized its earlier annals.

At this time passed the Test Act, which required all persons, before entering upon any public office, to take the oath of allegiance and supremacy, and receive the sacrament in the Established Church. They were also obliged to abjure all belief in the doctrine of transubstantiation. The effect of this Act was to exclude every conscientious Nonconformist from all public offices. The condition of their enjoyment involved a violation of their principles and an infringement of their creed, to take the sacrament in the Established Church. Thus was inflicted on Dissenters the gross injustice of exclusion from public employment, except upon terms which their conscience repelled. Their subsequent history proves how nobly the Dissenters obeyed the voice of conscience rather than the instinct of temporal interest and worldly gain. In their annals few were found who sacrificed their principles to gain the honour and emolument of public trust. Most of them clung to their profession, and despised the gold and distinction which could only be acquired by trampling on their Bible and their faith.

This measure was perhaps principally intended for the exclusion of the Papists from the places of public trust, but its provisions equally comprised the Dissenters. The Papists, though favoured by the King, were highly obnoxious to the parliament, whose measures were pregnant with extreme severity against this party; and this feeling it must be confessed was shared by the Dissenters nearly if not fully as much as by the Established Church. The Dissenters, though they complained of the injustice of being persecuted for their religion and faith, rejoiced to see the lash applied to the Papist to compel him to recant his creed. The scourge which they deemed so unjust to themselves they thought commendable against the Catholic. They even went farther, and refused toleration to themselves if it were thereby granted to the Papist, they rejected liberty for themselves if its acceptance involved freedom to the Catholic. With inconsistency like this do we find the best of men chargeable, in their conduct towards those whom they consider heretics or religious foes.

The absurdity of this Test Act consisted in prescribing the performance of religious rites as condition to the enjoyment of civil trust, because they are perfectly distinct, and have no connection necessary or political. Religion has its own domain, so has civil government; and they do not coalesce or even dovetail into one another, but like two great continents are separated by broad boundaries. The religious man may be a very incompetent civilian, and the illustrious civilian may be a very indifferent religionist. As just would it have been to have required the religious teacher before entering on his ministry to take an oath affirming the divine right of kings to rule, as to have obliged the civic functionary to testify to the king's supremacy and take the sacrament before entering on the duties of his office. But, though the requirement is absurd, it becomes criminal when it invades religious scruple; it is then pregnant with persecution, and establishes a principle which if carried out would annihilate religious liberty in the earth.

Charles was succeeded by his brother James, Duke of York, with the title of James the Second. James, less cautious and politic than his predecessor, had long before his assumption of the British crown avowed himself a Papist. On his accession he made a public avowal of his religious creed, and proceeded systematically to use his authority and influence for its propagation. He attended mass and other Roman Catholic services openly, and with all the ensigns of royal dignity. He sent Caryl as his agent to Rome, to propose a readmission of England into the Romish church. The pope, Innocent XIV., more prudent and wary than the King, advised him not to be too precipitate in his measures for the union of England and Rome, nor rashly attempt what would in all probability be impracticable. James afterwards went so far in countenancing popery as to admit one Father Petre, a jesuit, to a seat at his council board. The King filled the highest offices in the government with Catholic noblemen, and in all his measures the advancement of popery appears to have been his principal object. This he did not conceal, and the means which he adopted for effecting his purpose were as bold as manifest. Popery found in James a faithful ally, if not a prudent friend.

James, while zealous for popery, was intolerant towards other sects. Unable to conceal his hostility under the mask of hypocrisy he waged open war with other religious parties. The Nonconformists were peculiar objects of his animosity, and they suffered extreme persecution in the early part of his reign. He attempted to revive all the penal laws which his despotic predecessors had passed against religion, to advance popery, and eradicate protestantism. That infamous tribunal, the High Commission Court, which had been abolished by the long parliament, was now attempted to be re-established. Although this court had been abolished by act of parliament, James, regardless of that fact, treated the statute as still operative and issued an ecclesiastical commission whereby seven commissioners were vested with unlimited authority over the Church of England. Upon them were bestowed the same inquisitorial powers as were possessed by the former court when in its pristine glory. They might proceed upon bare suspicion, and they were expressly empowered to exercise their jurisdiction notwithstanding any law or statute to the contrary. Their authority was therefore absolute, and the intent was manifest. It was not doubted by the nation that the King's intention by this measure was to suppress protestantism and to raise to supremacy his favourite popery.

One of the most remarkable traits in this prince's character was inconsistency; from one extreme he suddenly rebounded to the other. Finding that a warfare so violent and undisguised against protestantism did not accomplish his ends, he altered his policy and became tolerant and friendly. Using that dangerous and unconstitutional power which his predecessors had frequently exercised, that of suspending the operation of penal statutes, James issued a proclamation suspending all the penal laws in ecclesiastical affairs, and granting general liberty of conscience to all his subjects. The design of this proclamation was to favour the Papists, who equally with the Dissenters were obnoxious to the penal laws against religion; and the wing whose protection was intended for the Papists only cast its shadow over the Dissenters equally. They found shelter under the enemy's roof. By an act so unconstitutional, proceeding from so sinister a motive, did the Dissenters procure the abrogation of the laws which for centuries had harassed their religious path. Now they were delivered from the oppression of ages, and well did they employ their liberty; their devotional meetings were now publicly held, and rapid was the progress of their sects. The winter of their sufferings was past, and the summer of their freedom had arrived.

The religious parties the most opposed to each other at this time were the Churchmen and Papists; the Nonconformists forming a third party, whose number and influence being considerable were courted by both the other parties and by the King as head of the Papists. The Dissenters sided with neither party farther than they saw that their adhesion to the one or the other advanced their religious liberty. They snatched the treasure which they sought, while their opponents were engaged in their conflict. They took advantage of the divisions among the rivals to bear away the prize of their freedom. But when James solicited their active concurrence in forwarding his measures for introducing popery and despotic power, he found the Nonconformists of this period not to belie their predecessors' memory, and to be still ready to form a phalanx of opposition to his designs. He therefore called them " an ill natured set who could not be gained."

Among other acts of imprudence James sent publicly the Earl of Castlemaine, his ambassador extraordinary, to Rome, to express his obeisance to the Pope, and to negotiate the reunion of his kingdom with the Romish power. This mission was treated by the Pope with indifference or even neglect, because the more wary Pontiff saw the imprudence of the step and the impracticability of the scheme. The only proof of regard for the mission which the Pontiff manifested was his sending a nuncio to the British court in return for the embassy. Any communication with the Pope was by act of parliament declared treason ; yet James, in defiance of this law and the feelings and opinions of his subjects, gave the nuncio a public reception at Windsor. This dignitary thenceforth during the remainder of this reign resided in London. Four Catholic bishops were publicly consecrated in the King's chapel, and sent out into different parts of the kingdom to exercise their episcopal functions. Their pastoral letters to the lay Catholics of England were printed and dispersed by the express permission of the King. The Catholic clergy appeared at court in the vestments of their order, and were patronised and honoured by James. Among other inroads upon the privileges of the Church by the Catholics, James recommended by mandate Father Francis, a Benedictine, to the degree of Master of Arts in the university of Cambridge, and one Farmer, a Catholic, to the office of President of Magdalen College, Oxford. These attempts at encroachment on the privileges of the universities were frustrated by the resistance of the college authorities.

The King, irritated by the opposition of the Church to his measures, was determined to confirm the toleration granted to the Dissenters from its communion. In the year 1688 James published a second declaration of indulgence in terms nearly similar to the former. He ordered that this declaration should, immediately after Divine service, be read by the clergy in all the churches. As the clergy denied and opposed the power assumed by the King of dispensing with penal laws, and were desirous of conciliating the people, who also felt hostility to the assumption of this prerogative, they determined to disobey the order. For their encouragement in this resolution six prelates (viz. Lloyd, Bishop of St. Asaph; Ken, of Bath and Wells; Turner, of Ely; Lake, of Chichester; White, of Peterborough; and Trelawney, of Bristol) petitioned the King against the order. This petition, which was mildly worded, complained not of the liberty which was granted to the Dissenters, but of the unconstitutional power which the King assumed in dispensing with penal enactments. They therefore besought the King not to insist upon the clergy reading the declaration in their churches. James, incensed by the remonstrance of the bishops, caused them to be committed to the Tower and prosecuted for the seditious libel alleged to be contained in their petition. The bishops were tried for their alleged offence, but acquitted by the jury.

James, by his systematic and unceasing efforts in favour of popery, and his exercise of the power of dispensing with the penal laws of the realm, had offended the nation at large. They saw that his attachment to popery was so extreme that he would neglect no opportunity and spare no effort to secure its supremacy within his dominions. They also saw the danger to their liberties arising from the exercise by the King of so despotic a power as that of suspending the operation of penal statutes. They perceived that both these tendencies were likely to lead the King to the commission of grave outrages in Church and State. They were therefore alarmed for their security and freedom.

In this situation their eyes were directed to William, Prince of Orange, who by his mother was nephew and by his wife was son-in-law of the King. They saw in the Prince the deliverer of his kingdom, the Netherlands, from the tyrannous encroachments of popery. They found him the champion of protestantism and the friend of liberty. The Churchman hailed the Prince as a fitting leader to deliver him from the dominion of a popish king; the Dissenter welcomed him as a monarch who would secure his peace and enlarge the charter of his freedom; the layman regarded him as a friend to the rights and liberties of man. Churchmen, Dissenters, and the laity therefore joined in inviting the Prince to come over and effect their deliverance from a popish king and arbitrary ruler. The Prince, whose ambition lagged not behind his ability and prowess, was not averse to the entreaty, and was not long before accepting the invitation. To pave the way for his expedition the Prince transmitted a declaration, which was published, "promising to endeavour a good agreement between the Church of England and Protestant Dissenters, and to come and secure all those who would live peaceably under the government from all persecution on account of their religion." He assured the Church party that he well regarded their religion, and that his education in Holland had nowise prejudiced him against episcopal government. The Dissenters he encouraged with promise of a full toleration and freedom of religious worship. The advent of the Prince of Orange was therefore regarded by Churchmen and Dissenters with interest and delight; the layman no less joined in the gratulation. At length the Prince's fleet set sail, and, wafted by friendly breezes, it anchored at Torbay, where the Prince and his forces landed on the fourth day of November, 1688. In his advance to meet the King's army, the Prince was joined by multitudes who flocked to his standard. Several counties of England took up arms in his cause, while the King was abandoned by the friends who first marched with him, and his army was daily diminishing by discontent and desertion. At last, finding success hopeless, James abdicated the throne and retired to France. The Prince of Orange was then invested with the British crown and sceptre by the representatives of the nation, and with the full approval of the people. Henceforth commenced the reign of William and Mary, and with it arose the dayspring of religious liberty and right.

William's religious views were liberal, his desire for freedom of creed and worship strong. This disposition of the King was much strengthened by his education in Holland. He there saw toleration carried out to its widest extent, and that no evil or inconvenience followed the indulgence. He there saw parties the most opposite in their religious creeds dwell together in harmony and peace. The freedom produced no discord, and the interests of the State suffered not by the indulgence. On the contrary, the harmonious feeling which pervaded the religious sects of that country, combined with their zeal and purity of conduct, must have endeared to William the principle of toleration which was their common bond. William therefore carried with him to England that quality which this country most needed, a spirit of toleration of all religious sects.

As he had, before his expedition was undertaken, vouchsafed to the Dissenters the promise of freedom of religion, they after his accession to the throne were not slow in calling for its performance. Nor was he averse to its fulfilment, and William's efforts for the emancipation of Dissenters from the tyranny of unjust laws and penal enactments are among the crowning events of his history.

One of William's first efforts in favour of Nonconformists was an attempt to abolish the sacramental test as a qualification for civil office. The King wished to open the door of preferment to the Dissenter as well as the Churchman, and that without violating his religious scruples. This wish of the King was intimated to both houses of parliament in the following words: "As I doubt not but you will sufficiently provide against Papists, so I hope you will have room for the admission of all Protestants who are willing and able to serve. This conjunction will tend to the better uniting you among yourselves, and the strengthening you against your common adversaries." A motion was therefore made in the House of Lords, on the discussion of the bill for abrogating the oaths of allegiance and supremacy, for the introduction into that measure of a clause abolishing the use of the sacrament as a qualification for any civil office or place of trust. Though sanctioned by the King, the clause was lost on a division by a considerable majority. William, in no wise discouraged by this ill success, was resolved to make another attempt for the accomplishment of his object. He therefore caused to be introduced another clause, providing that a person should be sufficiently qualified for any office, employment, or place of trust, who, within a year before or after his admission thereunto, did receive the sacrament of the Lord's supper, either in the Church of England or any other Protestant place of worship, and could produce a certificate thereof under the hands of the minister and two members of any such Protestant congregation. This clause met with the same result as the former one, being rejected by a large majority of the peers. The King was therefore constrained by the bigotry of his imperial parliament to leave unbroken those fetters which precluded the admission into civil offices of his Protestant dissenting subjects. William felt deeply the injustice of this exclusion, and his whole conduct as regards religious freedom shows that he was far in the advance of his parliament.

Baffled in these attempts for the emancipation of Nonconformists from this unjust restriction upon their civil and municipal rights, the King had nevertheless two important schemes for their benefit, which he afterwards proposed. The first was for the comprehension or alteration of the rubric of the Church of England in a manner somewhat conformable to the views of the Dissenters, so as thereby to induce them, or a large proportion of them, to unite with the Church of England; the other was for granting to Nonconformists full toleration of their religion and worship. In fulfilment of the scheme for a comprehension, a bill for uniting their majesties' Protestant subjects was introduced into the House of Lords. In the discussion on the bill a debate arose on the question of kneeling at the sacrament, which was yielded in favour of Dissenters. Another debate took place on the question "whether there should be an addition of laity on the commission to be given by the King to the bishops and others of the clergy for preparing such a reformation of ecclesiastical affairs as might be the means of healing divisions and correcting whatever might be erroneous or defective in the constitution." This addition was warmly supported by a great number of the temporal peers, and, when ultimately rejected, four of them entered their formal protest against the rejection. The bill itself was with some difficulty passed in the House of Lords, and it was then sent to the Commons, a majority of whom were hostile to the measure and treated it with neglect. Instead of proceeding with the bill the Commons presented an address to the King, thanking him for his gracious declaration and assurance that he would maintain the Church of England as by law established, and they humbly besought his majesty to issue writs for calling a convocation of the clergy, to be consulted on ecclesiastical matters according to the ancient usage of parliament, declaring at the same time that they would forthwith take into consideration proper methods for giving ease to Protestant Dissenters. The King, though displeased with the address, returned a civil answer, professing his regard for the Church of England, which should be always his peculiar care, recommending the Dissenters to their protection, and promising to summon a convocation as soon as such a measure should be necessary. Notwithstanding this reply, the Commons neglected the bill for a comprehension, which was accordingly not proceeded with.

Though disappointed again, the King was resolved to prosecute the scheme for a comprehension, in another form. In the next session William granted a commission under the great seal to ten bishops and twenty dignitaries of the Church, authorising them to meet from time to time in the Jerusalem Chamber, to prepare such alteration of the liturgy and canons, and such proposals for the reformation of ecclesiastical courts, as might most conduce to the good order, edification and uniting of the Church, and tend to reconcile all religious differences among his Protestant subjects. A loud outcry was raised against this commission, as creating a tribunal both illegal and dangerous. The fiercest in the opposition to the measure were the Bishops of Rochester and Winchester, and the Doctors Jane and Aldrich, who represented the commission as an authority for making such alterations in the liturgy and doctrines of the Church as would divide the clergy and bring the Church into disesteem with the people, as it would be a plain acknowledgment that it needed reformation. They also thought they should violate the dignity of the Church by making offers which the Dissenters were at liberty to refuse. These dignitaries, who were members of the commission, therefore retired from the meeting and refused to join in the proceedings under it; the rest of the commissioners notwithstanding prosecuted the commission. They discussed with moderation the abuses complained of by the Dissenters, and corrected such articles as seemed to them justly objectionable. The opponents of the measure were loud in their outcry against it, and the universities joined in the opposition. They denounced the King as an enemy of the hierarchy, and by their efforts they procured the election of a majority of their own party in the convocation. The reforming members of the convocation were further discouraged by the election of Dr. Jane, a violent dissentient, as prolocutor, in preference to Dr. Tillotson. A majority of the House of Commons was also opposed to the commission, and notwithstanding the zealous efforts and sagacious movement of the King to induce a different result, the commission became practically fruitless. The scheme for a comprehension of the Protestants of the empire was therefore again frustrated.

But William's efforts for a toleration of Dissenters met with a different result, they were triumphantly successful. On the 28th of February, 1689, the Earl of Nottingham presented a bill to the House of Lords, entitled "An Act to exempt their Majesties' Protestant subjects dissenting from the Church of England from the penalties of certain laws," which was passed through its various stages in both houses of parliament with little difficulty, and received the royal assent on the 24th of May, 1689. Some zealots in parliament proposed to give the bill a limited duration, in order, as they said, to test the deserts of the Dissenters, and to see whether at the expiration of that time their conduct would entitle them to its continuance; but this illiberal attempt was speedily frustrated by the general feeling of the house, and the Act accordingly had a permanent operation. It enacted that none of the penal laws should be construed to extend to the Dissenters, or to the preachers and teachers in congregations of dissenting Protestants, who should take the oath of allegiance to the reigning government, and subscribe the declaration prescribed in the thirtieth year of the reign of Charles II., of their belief in certain articles of the Christian faith; and that any person who should disturb a religious congregation in a church, chapel, or meeting house, should be liable to a penalty of £20, increased by 52 George III., cap. 155, to £40, recoverable before justices at quarter sessions.

Thus, after ages of persecution and suffering, the Nonconformists obtained their debt of justice, a toleration of their religion and worship. From the Reformation to the Revolution, a period of near one hundred and fifty years, with the exception of the short reign of Edward the Sixth and the Commonwealth era, the Dissenters of England endured the horrors of persecution. The reign of the successive monarchs were to them but one continued winter of suffering, each fresh accession but varying the phase of their woes. Their sufferings during this period were inconceivably great, but not greater than the fortitude of the Puritans. The Nonconformists of this era were suited to the times in which they lived; their zeal and heroism were equal to the storms they underwent. They were for the most part men who, before they publicly avowed their principles, had resolved to endure whatsoever consequences might follow their profession. They had not espoused their religion as a summer companion, but as an ally in life and death, whose cause was to be supported in its winter of adversity equally as in its season of prosperity. The union between them and their faith could not in their estimation be dissolved by death and the grave, but would thrive in eternity. They looked to immortality for the full fruition of its peace; then alone would its blessings be complete. This was to them, therefore, a treasure worth suffering for its acquisition; it was a pearl whose retention was worth enduring the direst of human pains. It consequently made them heroic; it elevated them beyond the terrors of death and the grave; it lifted them to immortality; it divested the prison, the scaffold and the stake of their horror, it converted them into ministers of hope and instruments of joy. Armed with its prowess, they dreaded not the power of man; fortified with its consolation they could look with indifference on the tempests that surrounded them. It was their succour in life, their comfort in death, and would be their ministering angel in eternity. Such were the men who obtained and preserved for Britain the proudest gem in the diadem of her glories, the ark of her civil and religious liberty.

William died on the 8th day of March, 1702, after a reign of thirteen years, which was distinguished alike by its warlike achievements, its civil grandeur, and its successful efforts for religious emancipation. He was succeeded by Anne, the younger daughter of James the Second by his queen, the daughter of the Earl of Clarendon. Departing from the path of her immediate predecessor, she early commenced hostilities against the dissenting community, and during the whole of her reign she waged relentless war against their liberty and rights. In this war she was stimulated and joined by the hierarchy of the Church of England as well as by many of the nobility and gentry who favoured her communion. In the two preceding reigns the Church of England and its supporters countenanced and befriended the Dissenters from selfish motives. During the reign of James the Second they saw the continued efforts of the King for the establishment of popery in England, and to ward off so inveterate a foe they thought it prudent to make peace with the Nonconformists, who were both numerous and powerful. They courted the Dissenters for the purpose of gaining their support in the opposition which was to be offered to the advances of the popish church. The Dissenters, merging all reminiscences of past sufferings in a regard for the success of truth and the defeat of error, joined the Church of England in its crusade against the insidious advances of Rome. By their united efforts the Prince of Orange was enabled to crush popery in England by the expulsion of James, its patron and leader. The reign of protestantism was established on a firm and lasting basis by the successful efforts of William and his parliament. There was no longer any fear of the ascendancy of popery, and the Church hierarchy felt secure in the enjoyment of their dignities and revenues. They felt they could dispense with the friendly assistance of the Dissenters, and the alliance was therefore severed. Previously, during the period of danger, the Dissenters were courted and caressed; now, in the hour of triumph and safety, they were shunned and despised. Theretofore, underneath the shield which they held out against popery, Dissenters might have plucked the richest favours which the King and parliament could bestow, and that with the full concurrence of the hierarchy; but now that the common foe was disarmed and a captive, the old enmity was to be revived, and the rancour of religious bigotry to be renewed. Henceforth the Church was at liberty to pursue its old course for the extermination of dissent.

In the first year of the Queen's reign a bill was introduced into the House of Commons for preventing occasional conformity. In the preamble all persecution for conscience sake was condemned, while the subsequent part had the following provision: that all those who had taken the sacrament and test for offices of trust or the magistracy of corporations, and afterwards frequented any meeting of Dissenters where there should be five besides the family, should be disabled from holding their employments, pay a fine of £100, and £5 for every day in which they continued to act in such employments after having been at such meeting. They were also rendered incapable of holding any other public employment till after one whole year's conformity to the Established Church, and upon a relapse the fines and incapacity were doubled. The object of this bill was to completely exclude all Nonconformists from every public employment or place. Many of the Dissenters, especially Presbyterians, had since the passing of the Test Act accepted court offices and taken the required sacramental test, although they afterwards attended the worship of the Dissenting communion of which they previously were members. This occasional conformity formed not so considerable an objection to the presbyterian as to the other dissenting bodies, for many among the former occasionally attended the worship and service of the Church of England. On the accession of Anne, therefore, many Nonconformists filled the public offices of the country with honour and advantage to the community; and to deprive such of their places or to compel their union with the Church, and to prevent the admission of Dissenters into such offices in future, were the objects of this bill. It was a further step, in the direction of the Test Act, for restricting the liberties of Nonconformists, and demolishing their civil and municipal rights. A measure so iniquitous met, as may be supposed, warm opposition in its progress, but so impregnated was the House of Commons of this period with religious bigotry that the bill passed by a considerable majority. It received violent opposition in the House of Lords, and among those who distinguished themselves by opposing the measure in that house was a number of bishops, constituting a majority of that order. The bill was after stormy debates amended by that house, lowering the penalty from £100 to £20, one third to go to the Queen, another third to the poor, and the last to the informer. The clause imposing a fine of £5 a day for the continuance in office after forfeiture, and all the subsequent parts of the bill which related to future incapacity for office, were left out, and several mitigating clauses were added. These amendments, on being submitted to the House of Commons, were refused, whereupon a conference took place between deputies from both houses. The result was the adhesion of the Lords and the refusal of the Commons to the amendments, and the bill was lost. Thus for the present did this iniquitous attempt on the rights of Nonconformists prove abortive, but the venom still remained in the breast of its abettors, and they wanted but a fitting opportunity for its emission.

In the parliament which met in the following

year the bill was a second time introduced into the Lower House, but to disarm opposition it was altered in some important parts. Instead of five beside the family, as in the former bill, ten was now necessary to form a conventicle. The penalty of £100 was reduced to £50, and the clause inflicting the fine of £5 a day for continuance in office after forfeiture was left out. The bill met with strong opposition, but was carried by a considerable majority, and sent up to the Lords, where it was rejected by a majority of twelve.

Though twice defeated, the Tories were determined to proceed with the bill. In the next session, which begun in October 1704, the Bill was a third time introduced into the Lower House and passed. It was then proposed to tack it to a money bill and send it up to the Lords, that it might thus be secure from alteration in that house; but this was negatived by a large majority, and it was at length sent up as a distinct bill. The debates in the Upper House took place in the presence of the Queen, who attended to hear them. On the second reading the bill was thrown out by a majority of twenty-one. Thus thrice during this period did the imperial parliament prove itself to be the opponent of aggression and the upholder of the rights of conscience; and, highly to their honour, among the guardians of liberty on this occasion were a considerable number of bishops, comprising Burnet, who signalised himself by his candid and enlightened opposition.

The bill was now laid aside, and the Nonconformists were for several years unmolested by any attempt for its revival. But the old wish remained in the breast of its promoters, and more fitting times to renew the project afterwards arrived. The advent of these times was prepared by the trial and punishment of Henry Sacheverell, the champion of high church and tory principles. The result of these transactions was the supplanting of the Whig by a Tory ministry, and the ascendancy of extreme principles in both Church and State. At length the Earl of Nottingham, a recent deserter from the Tories to the Whigs, introduced into the House of Lords a bill entitled "An Act for preserving the Protestant Religion by better securing the Church of England, and for continuing the Toleration granted to Protestant Dissenters by an Act for supplying the defects thereof." Under a title so amicable were couched provisions so fierce and heinous as the following: "any person who filled an office or place of trust and profit under government, or common councilmen in corporations, who should be present at any meeting for Divine worship when there were more than ten persons besides the family, in which the liturgy was not used, should upon conviction forfeit the said office and place of trust and profit, and continue incapable of enjoying any such situation until he should be able to make oath that he had not been present at any conventicle during a whole year, and in that time had at least thrice received the Lord's supper according to the rites and usage of the Church of England." A considerable number of the Whig peers having been won over by the Earl of Nottingham to support the bill, it passed the House of Lords and afterwards the House of Commons, and in its progress a clause was added imposing a penalty of £40, on conviction of the offence of being at a conventicle, to be paid to the informer. The French and Dutch Protestants petitioned to be heard against the bill, but no attention was paid to the request. Thus, after so many previous failures, was this infamous encroachment on the rights and liberties of Nonconformists carried, and the hideous provisions of the bill against occasional conformity were added to the statute book to dishonour its pages.

The usual policy of the Church and Tory party for the extermination of dissent was to prevent the children of Dissenters receiving any education excepting such as inculcated the doctrines of the Church of England; by this means it was supposed nonconformity would be nearly or entirely extinct in the next generation. The design was as inju-

H

rious as iniquitous. A bill having this object was introduced into the House of Commons on the 12th of May, 1714, which proposed to enact "that no person should keep any public or private school or seminary, to teach or instruct youth as tutor or schoolmaster, unless he subscribed this declaration, 'I, A. B., do declare that I will conform to the liturgy of the Church of England as by law established,' and shall have had or obtained a licence from the archbishop, bishop, or ordinary of the place under the seal of office." Whosoever should be found doing so without these qualifications was upon conviction to suffer three months' imprisonment. No licence was to be granted unless the candidate produced a certificate that he had received the sacrament according to the usage of the Church of England at some parish church, within the year. If after this the schoolmaster should be present at a conventicle or any other worship than that of the Church of England, he should be liable to three months' imprisonment, and from thenceforth be incapable of teaching in any school or seminary, or instructing any youth as tutor or schoolmaster. Another clause was: "if any person licensed as aforesaid shall teach any other catechism than the catechism set forth in the Book of Common Prayer, the licence of such person shall from henceforth be void, and such person shall be liable to the penalties of this Act." A person who had lost his licence for any of the causes mentioned in the bill must, in order to resume his competency of acting as schoolmaster or tutor, be able to make oath in a court of justice that during twelve months he had not been present at any conventicle for dissenting worship, and had received the sacrament during the year according to the usage of the Church of England. This iniquitous measure was called the Schism Bill. It was vigorously opposed in the House of Commons by some of the leading members, but was eventually carried by a majority of 267 against 126 votes. It was then sent to the House of Lords, where it received a still more powerful opposition, but the third reading was carried by a majority of 77 against 72 votes. Some mitigating clauses were however added in the latter house. One was that the Dissenters might be permitted to have schoolmistresses to teach their children to read, and another that the Act should not extend to any person who should instruct youth in reading, writing, arithmetic, or any part of mathematical learning which related to navigation, or any mechanical art only. This infamous Act received the royal assent on the 29th of June, 1714, and was to come into operation on the 1st day of August following; but on the latter day the Queen died, and with her death the spirit of religious persecution in the British monarch ceased, and her sceptre was resigned to a family who have invariably proved themselves to be the friends and abettors of the civil and religious liberty of the subject. The Act against Schism was therefore never enforced, but remained obsolete on the statute book until the stain of its existence was wiped away by its repeal.

Notwithstanding the severity of the measures which were passed against it during the reign of Queen Anne, nonconformity prospered. Under the genial shade of William's administration it had much increased, and it was found to survive the persecuting shocks of the following reign, multiplied and strengthened. Previous history should have taught monarchs and their advisers the insufficiency of persecution to extinguish truth, and this reign added its testimony to the important fact. The Nonconformists of this period included Presbyterians, Independents, Baptists, and Quakers. The numerical strength of the parties was in the order indicated, the Presbyterians being the most numerous. They all together formed a powerful phalanx for the preservation of liberty civil and religious, which inestimable treasure they transmitted to modern times. In all the ages at which we have glanced, the civil liberty of the subject was fostered and preserved in the ranks of puritanism and nonconformity alone. It was in this soil that the precious plant grew and flourished. Here was its proper bed, beside its handmaid, religious freedom. They grew together; for their twin birth and nurture there was a moral necessity. The curator of religious freedom must have been the guardian of civil liberty. He found them associated, and like two empresses ruling over kingdoms whose boundaries overlapped each other. He could not have secured the one without the other, for as the limits of the one empire became evanescent in the dominions of the other, after he took the one under his tutelage he must have taken both. The abettor of religious freedom has therefore in all ages been the defender of civil liberty; the religious reformer has consequently been invariably the civil patriot. Both characters spring from the same root, and are fed by the same sap and moisture. The leaders of the two great revolutions at whose transactions we have glanced, viz. Cromwell and the Prince of Orange, furnish an illustration of this truth. They blended the religious liberator with the civil reformer, their power was founded on the double stratification, they were heroes of the two great principles we have named *together*, and not of the one alone. Their empire had therefore double strength, and ought to have had double permanence.

On the death of Anne the house of Brunswick acceded to the throne in the person of George the

First. The implacable enemies of religious freedom, the Tories, were now supplanted by the Whigs, who have always proved themselves the friends of toleration. This augured well for the interests of nonconformity, and the events of this reign realized the blessings anticipated. The King himself was high in the esteem of the Dissenters, and his accession to the throne was welcomed by their community. Addresses of congratulation were presented to him on their behalf, and public prayer was made in their meeting houses for his welfare and safety. The King on the other hand was well affected towards Nonconformists, and the whole tenor of his reign showed his desire to break their fetters and establish their freedom. One of the earliest measures of his reign was for the relief of Quakers. By a statute passed in the reign of King William III., the affirmation of this people was in civil causes declared equivalent to an oath, to which they had a conscientious objection. But the Act was made to endure for a limited time, that its effects might be ascertained, and, if injurious, that the statute itself might be no longer continued. But early in this reign this indulgence to the Quakers was continued and confirmed by parliamentary statute. Thus was a pledge given, by those in power, to extend favour to the Nonconformists.

Perceiving this disposition of the King and the

ministry, the Dissenters were determined to avail themselves of the favourable conjuncture, and to seek for the abrogation of some of the severest laws which had been passed against them. No statutes infringed their rights more than those passed in the previous reign against occasional conformity and schism, and the Corporation and Test Acts. The Dissenters were therefore determined to commence their attack upon this portion of the citadel of oppression. In this resolve they were encouraged by the King's speech to his parliament at the opening of the session, 1717, wherein he said: "I could heartily wish that, at a time when the enemies of our religion are by all manner of artifices endeavouring to undermine and weaken it both at home and abroad, all those who are friends to our present happy establishment might unanimously concur in some proper method for the greater strengthening the Protestant interest of which, as the Church of England is unquestionably the main support and bulwark, so will she reap the principal benefits of every advantage accruing by the union and mutual charity of all Protestants. As none can recommend themselves more effectually to my favour than by a sincere zeal for the just rights of the crown and the liberties of the people, so I am determined to encourage all those who act agreeably to the constitution of these my kingdoms, and consequently to the principles on which my government is founded." The Dissenters had resolved to present their claim before parliament for a repeal of the Test and Corporation Acts, as well as those against occasional conformity and schism; but on the assurance of their friends in parliament that to compass the repeal of the Test and Corporation Acts in the proposed bill would be to frustrate the whole measure they prudently abandoned, for the time being, the onslaught on those laws. A bill to repeal the Occasional Conformity and Schism Acts was on the 13th of December, 1718, introduced into the House of Lords, under the title of "An Act for strengthening the Protestant interest in these kingdoms." It also proposed to repeal some of the clauses in the Test and Corporation Acts. The bill was violently opposed by a number of the peers, and particularly the bishops, who were loud in their outcry against it; but it passed, with the exception of the clauses relating to the Test and Corporation Acts, which were voluntarily abandoned. The bill was then sent to the Commons, where it was carried by a considerable majority, and became law on the 18th of February, 1719. Thus were abrogated those severe laws against Nonconformists which were enacted by the bigotry of the preceding reign. Among those who distinguished themselves by their advocacy of this relieving Act in parliament were

Dr. Hoadley, Bishop of Bangor, and Dr. Kennet, Bishop of Peterborough. Notwithstanding the virulent antagonism of their mitred brethren, these prelates fearlessly stood forward to vindicate the rights of religion and conscience, and their righteous appeals were crowned with success.

But the thirst of bigotry and intolerance would not be quenched without resistance; the hydra would not be crushed without a struggle. Taking advantage of the publication of some pamphlets at this period, which were alleged to be productive of infidelity and irreligion, the Dean of Windsor brought into the Upper House a bill for the more effectual suppression of blasphemy and profaneness. It enacted that any person who should by advised speaking deny certain doctrines contained in the thirty-nine articles of the Church of England should, in addition to the penalties inflicted by an Act of William the Third against blasphemy, be imprisoned for several months, unless he should renounce his error and make a certain profession of his faith; and, further, that if any preacher in any separate congregation should by writing or advised speaking deny any fundamental articles of the Christian religion, he should be deprived of the benefits of the Toleration Act. Moreover, the justices of the peace were empowered to summon any such preacher, or any person called a Quaker, to appear before them and to subscribe the declaration of his belief contained in the Act, or be denied the benefit of toleration. Thus another attempt was made at the foundation of man's religious belief by parliamentary statute, and another essay at the impossible task of prescribing to the human mind, by legislative enactment, the measure and quality of its thoughts. But parliament had made some advance in metaphysical science since the reigns of Mary and Elizabeth, and perceived the impracticability of such a scheme. They seem now to have abandoned that prerogative which in previous reigns was so fondly cherished, of endeavouring to direct man *how* and *what* he should think of his Maker, and of himself in relation to Him! The bill for the suppression of blasphemy and profaneness was rejected by a large majority.

This reign abounded in favour to Quakers. They complained that the form of affirmation which was already prescribed for their adoption amounted to an oath. The words to which they objected were these, "in the presence of Almighty God." They therefore petitioned parliament for its alteration. A bill was accordingly introduced and passed, fulfilling their wish. The words referred to were ordered by the Act to be excluded from their affirmation, and in lieu thereof it was to commence with the words, "I solemnly, sincerely, and truly affirm and declare." This sect was therefore loud in its commendation of this reign, and in its attachment to the ruling power, and they united with the other dissenting bodies in a steadfast support of the crown.

Another minor measure for the relief of Dissenters which passed during this reign was an Act for repealing a clause in an Act of the 12th year of Queen Anne, which declared that no person should be capable of being a guardian of the poor in the city of Bristol, who should not have taken the sacrament according to the rites of the Church of England. This clause, which excluded Dissenters from the office in question, was repealed. The Dissenters were the more rejoiced at this Act, because they regarded it as an earnest of the eventual repeal of those more general and oppressive laws under which they laboured, the Test and Corporation Acts.

The progress of nonconformity during this reign was considerable. Under the favourable auspices of the government it increased and strengthened. Enjoying royal countenance, it appeared the more attractive to many, while others were induced to join its ranks because the fears of persecution were ended. But many more swelled the number of its followers from their love of its doctrines, and who would have entered its pale although the storm of persecution had still continued to roll over its people. The prejudice against dissent which the royal discountenance and parliamentary hostility of former reigns could not fail to have engendered had now passed away, and its followers were looked upon, by those in authority and station, with a more candid and dispassionate eye. They were now seen to be neither seditious in politics nor fanatics in religion. It was perceived that their theological creed diminished not their usefulness either as citizens or subjects, but that on the contrary it was productive of a purity in their conduct and a conscientiousness in their dealings which were highly commendable. It was also seen that the tenets which they held were neither dangerous nor absurd, and violated not the Bible or reason. Dissenters therefore acquired in this reign a civic importance which they had not previously enjoyed except during the Commonwealth. They were no longer branded as insurgents or denounced as heretics, but were recognised in society as persons deserving its respect. Enjoying toleration from the law, favour from the monarch, and protection from the parliament, the Nonconformists waxed strong, and deep in the conviction of the purity of their faith they looked to the future with confidence and joy.

On the death of George the First, which took place

on his way to Hanover on the 11th of June, 1727, the sceptre descended to his son, George the Second. The young King was a favourite of the Dissenters, who in anticipation had invested him with that liberality towards their sect which his father had invariably shown. They had supposed that the son would inherit with the crown those virtues with which it was associated when on the father's brow; particularly those virtues which are the result of training and example more than of natural gifts. Nor in this were they disappointed. The young King filled the measure of his father's liberality. Liberty of conscience and the right of private judgment in religion were the principles which imbued his reign. The dawn of religious freedom had commenced in his father's administration, it was now advancing towards a meridian light.

The old spirit of intolerance was nevertheless not dead, and it pervaded a portion of the legislative assembly; it dwelt strongly in the bosom of the Church. A convocation of the clergy in the beginning of this reign attempted to revive the claims of the Church to dictate the religious creed of the people. A member of that assembly, addressing the prolocutor, said: "As his majesty has answered the late address of both Houses with an assurance that he will be ready on his part towards a rigorous execution of the law against profaneness, blasphemy, and immorality, it will doubtless be more effectually accomplished if the Church representative, that is to say, convocation, points out to him what persons or things are most likely to promote or impede his royal and pious design. . . . It cannot be deemed unreasonable for any dutiful son or servant both of the Church and State then to loose his tongue-strings, when the several parts and offices of our holy religion are exposed to mockery, and the doctrines and mysteries of religion are furiously attacked by men of profligate principles." He then proposed that the Deists and Socinians should be struck dumb by an awful censure from the convocation. The King perceived the design of this manifesto, and would not be diverted from the path of toleration which his father's example had recommended and in which he himself had hitherto trod. The convocation was therefore frustrated in its object of overriding the consciences of men, and had to mourn in silence the clemency of the times.

In the Act of King William the Third, which continued the privilege of affirmation to the Quakers, clauses were contained authorising a cheaper and more summary method of recovering tithes and churchrates of small amount from the Quakers, who had a conscientious objection to the imposts and frequently withheld payment until recovered by process of law; but as this Act left it optional to the clergy to adopt that method, or the more expensive one in the superior law and ecclesiastical courts, the clergy, to harass the Quakers, the more frequently pursued the latter course. The Friends, justly resenting this oppressive choice, petitioned parliament, setting forth their grievances. A bill was accordingly introduced into the House of Commons, compelling the clergy to adopt the less expensive process of law for recovery of their tithes from the Quakers. Notwithstanding the reasonableness of the measure, the clergy violently declaimed against it, assigning no other reason for their opposition than that they wished to preserve the power of resorting to the more expensive method of law to punish the Quakers. The bill however passed the House of Commons. In the Upper House the reasons for the measure were so irresistible that no opposition was offered to its general principles; but the opponents of religious liberty in that House, taking advantage of a technical defect in the bill as it had passed the Lower House, caused its miscarriage, and it was thrown out. The power of the clergy to oppress the Quakers by expensive lawsuits was therefore preserved.

Countenanced by the King, the Dissenters made

attempts for the repeal of the clauses in the Test Act which debarred them from admission into civil employments of a public nature. A motion to this effect was made in the House of Commons in the early part of the year 1736, but was negatived by a majority of that assembly. The motion was renewed in the following session, but met with the same result. The Nonconformists were therefore obliged to continue under a restriction which excluded them from civil offices to which they had an indefeasible right as citizens and subjects. Although the King himself was more enlightened, his parliament does not appear to have made any advance in political wisdom. The clouds of bigotry which in previous ages had obscured the eyes of legislators do not appear, even at this late period, to have left the halls of the senate; the gloom still covered that elevated assembly, darkened its counsels, and poisoned its decrees.

During this reign and the next lived John Wesley, the founder of Methodism. Educated in the university of Oxford, where at Lincoln College he was fellow and tutor, he was ordained for the ministry of the Established Church. Being dissatisfied with the lethargy of its ministers, and inflamed with zeal for the conversion of mankind, he in the year 1739 began to teach and preach outside the pale of the Establishment. In this holy work he was joined by his brother Charles, and afterwards by George Whitefield, the Apollos of the day. These early apostles of Methodism at first professed allegiance to the Established Church, of which they continued to be members, and ministered in the highways and hedges of the world to bring sinners into the same ecclesiastical fold; but eventually they left its pale, and themselves separated, John Wesley becoming the founder of Arminian or Wesleyan Methodism, and Whitefield of Calvinistic Methodism. The arduous labours of these zealous and self denying ministers of Christ were eminently successful in England and America, where (and in the British colonies) their followers constitute the most numerous and flourishing of the dissenting bodies.

George the Second died on the 25th of October, 1760, in the thirty-third year of his reign, and was succeeded by his grandson George the Third, who extended the same protection and showed the same favour to Nonconformists which his royal forefathers had done. In the year 1772 a significant petition to parliament was presented from several hundred ministers of the Established Church, and numerous lay members, containing the following memorable expressions, viz.: "We apprehend that we have certain rights and privileges which we hold of God alone, one of which

I

is the exercise of our own reason and judgment. We are also warranted by those original principles of the reformation from popery, on which the Church of England is founded, to judge in searching the Scriptures, each man for himself, what may or may not be proved thereby. From the enjoyment of this valuable privilege we find ourselves in a great measure precluded by the laws relative to subscription, requiring us to acknowledge certain articles and confessions of faith and doctrines, drawn up by fallible men, to be all and every one of them agreeable to the sacred Scriptures. We request to be freed from these impositions, and to be restored to our undoubted right, as Protestants, of interpreting the Scriptures for ourselves, without being bound by any human explanations, a submission to which is an encroachment on our rights both as men and as members of a Protestant establishment."

After several unsuccessful attempts, an Act was passed in 1779 relieving dissenting ministers and Nonconformists generally from subscribing to the articles prescribed by the Toleration Act, and the following unobjectionable declaration was substituted: "I, A. B., do solemnly declare in the presence of Almighty God that I am a Christian and a Protestant, and as such that I believe that the Scriptures of the Old and New Testament, as commonly received among Protestant churches, do contain the revealed will of God, and that I do receive the same as the rule of my doctrine and practice."

The Roman Catholics (who numbered some of the highest personages and largest proprietors in the kingdom) were up to this time obnoxious to severer laws than Nonconformists. These, among other things, prescribed that "popish priests and jesuits found officiating in the services of their church shall be guilty of felony." A Catholic educated abroad lost his estate, and Papists were incapable of acquiring real property. On the motion of that eminent and virtuous Protestant senator, Sir George Saville, a bill repealing these cruel laws passed the House of Commons and afterwards the Lords, and like every other measure of relief and religious toleration graciously received the royal assent.

Lord Sidmouth made an insidious but abortive attempt against Nonconformist preaching, by introducing into the House of Lords, on the 21st of May, 1811, a bill restricting the privileges of the Toleration Acts to ministers of separate churches and congregations, and subjecting itinerant preachers to the penal laws; the object having been, as he stated, to prevent the national danger of a "nominal established church and a sectarian people"; but the whole dissenting community vigorously united to oppose the bill, and in forty-eight hours six hundred petitions, signed by a hundred thousand males, were presented to the Peers against it. The bill was also denounced in terms so eloquent and forcible by Lords Erskine, Holland, Grey, Stanhope, and others, that it was ordered to be read a second time that day six months. This was the last great parliamentary attempt to encroach upon the religious liberty of the English nation.

George the Third, the eminently Protestant King, died in the year 1820, after a prosperous reign of sixty years, and was succeeded by his son George the Fourth. After several unsuccessful efforts by previous senators, Lord John Russell, on the 26th of February, 1828, introduced into the House of Commons, in a most able and luminous speech, a bill to relieve Dissenters of the most obnoxious clauses in the Corporation and Test Acts, which after much argument and opposition was passed in a full house by a majority of forty-four votes. This measure, so triumphantly carried through the Lower House, was introduced to the Peers by Lord Holland in an equally convincing address, and passed after a warm controversy by a considerable majority, royalty afterwards giving its cordial assent. In this manner, after a period of two centuries during which these unjust and odious laws encumbered the statute book, **the** Nonconformists **of** Great Britain obtained their **repeal.** Thus, in **the** moral world as **in the material universe,** Providence eventually accomplishes justice and equity by the gradual development of natural laws.

After several previous attempts for Catholic emancipation, in which Messrs. Grattan, O'Conuell, and Shiel distinguished themselves, Mr. (afterwards Sir Robert) Peel, then Home Secretary, on the 5th of March, 1829, moved the introduction into the House of Commons of a bill to relieve Roman Catholics of the religious and political disabilities imposed on them in former reigns. This bill was strongly opposed and vehemently debated in both houses of parliament, but was carried by large majorities, and became law on the 12th of April, 1829. The same eminent statesman had previously the merit of introducing the bills called after him "Peel's Acts," which simplified and mitigated the severity of the criminal law of England, ably seconded by those philanthropic senators, Romilly and Mackintosh, who had long before forcibly impressed the legislature and people with the necessity for the change. The same illustrious statesman long afterwards, when First Lord of Her Majesty's Treasury, had the privilege of introducing a bill to repeal the duties on the importation into the United Kingdom of foreign corn, powerfully supported by the earlier apostles of free trade, Messrs. Villiers, Cobden, and Bright, and after strenuous opposition triumphantly carried. It is seldom that the good fortune of proposing for the adoption of the legislature, at long intervals, measures so important and beneficent as the mitigation of the criminal law, Catholic emancipation, and free trade should have devolved on one and the same senator.

On the death of George the Fourth his brother William ascended the throne on the 26th of June, 1830. In this reign was passed the Act 6 and 7 William IV., cap. 85, enabling the ministers of nonconformist chapels or places of religious worship to celebrate therein the rites or ceremonies of baptism and marriage, and legalising the registration thereof. This important concession has been extensively adopted by the Nonconformists, a great number of whose places of worship have been licensed for the solemnization of marriage.

William the Fourth died on the 20th of June, 1837, and was succeeded by our present good and gracious Queen, Victoria, who has ever since reigned over a prosperous and contented nation. Inheriting the just and liberal principles of her line, the royal house of Brunswick, she has bestowed her countenance and given her welcome assent to every measure which has been brought forward and passed by the legislature, erasing from the statute book the unjust and odious laws which the bigotry and intolerance of the Tudor and Stuart reigns had imposed on Nonconformists. Among these may be mentioned the removal of Jewish disabilities in 1858 and 1860, the repeal of the last shred of the Test and Corporation Acts in 1866, the abolition of compulsory churchrates in 1868, and of religious tests in the Universities in 1871. The modern Dissenter is as securely free to worship the God of his fathers, in his own fashion, in his own place of worship, as the Episcopalian in his parish church. All the modern Nonconformist wants, and this he will eventually have, is that the Episcopalian shall maintain his minister and place of worship by his own voluntary contribution, in like manner as the Dissenter, throughout the dark ages of sorrow and suffering, in adversity and prosperity, has liberally supported his own pastor and chapel.

The greater part of this paper was written more than thirty years ago, when the writer was young, and vigorous and active in the performance of professional duties, and at a time when the principles established by the English Reformation and Revolution were making steady and even rapid progress under the beneficent rule of a Liberal administration. At a later period the political and religious atmospheres have been much darkened by the ascendancy of high church and tory principles and parties, not only in England but in Germany and Austro-Hungary, which has produced a considerable reaction and retrogression throughout Europe. The writer therefore thought it his duty to restore a shelved manuscript, and contribute his small assistance and dim light to check this reaction and dispel this gloom, by reproducing to the rising generation an imperfect picture of those momentous times and gigantic struggles, through which, at so great a cost of suffering and blood, their forefathers achieved the precious conquest of civil and religious liberty.

A SUMMARY OF THE LAWS RELATING TO THE CONVEYANCE AND ENJOYMENT OF PUBLIC PLACES FOR RELIGIOUS WORSHIP AND ELEMENTARY EDUCATION.

CHAPTER II.

SO great a portion of the land of the country was being granted and given by owners, in some instances under undue influence, for religious and charitable uses and purposes, and thereby abstracting it from private ownership and enjoyment, that the legislature passed the Act of 9 George II., cap. 36, to restrain such conveyances and gifts, which has been most beneficial in its operation. Section 1 enacts that "after the 24th day of June, 1736, no lands or other hereditaments whatsoever, nor any sums of money or personal estate whatsoever to be laid out or disposed of in the purchase of any lands or hereditaments, should be given or any ways conveyed to any person or persons, bodies politic or corporate or otherwise, for any estate or interest whatsoever, in trust or for the benefit of any charitable uses whatsoever, unless such gift or conveyance of any such lands or hereditaments, sums of money or personal estate (other than stocks in the public funds), be made by deed executed in the presence of two or more credible witnesses, twelve calendar months before the death of such donor or grantor, including the days of the execution and death, and be enrolled in the Court of Chancery within six calendar months next after the execution thereof, and unless such stocks be transferred six calendar months before the death of such donor or grantor, including the days of transfer and death, and unless the same be made to take effect in possession for the charitable use intended immediately from the making thereof, and be without any power of revocation, reservation, trust, condition, limitation, or agreement whatsoever for the benefit of the donor or grantor, or of any person or persons claiming under him."

Section 2 provides " that nothing thereinbefore contained relating to the sealing and delivering of any deed twelve calendar months before the death of the grantor, or to the transfer of any stock six calendar months before the death of the grantor or person making such transfer, shall extend or be construed to extend to any purchase of any estate or interest in lands, tenements, or hereditaments, or any transfer of any stock to be made really and *bonâ fide* for a full and valuable consideration actually paid at or before the making of such conveyance or transfer without fraud or collusion."

Section 3 enacts " that all gifts, grants, conveyances, appointments, transfers, and settlements whatsoever of any land or other hereditaments, or of any estate or interest therein, or of any charge or incumbrance affecting any lands or hereditaments, or of any stocks, money, or other personal estate or securities for money to be laid out or disposed of in the purchase of any lands or hereditaments, or of any estate or interest therein, or of any charge or incumbrance affecting the same to or in trust for any charitable uses whatsoever, which shall at any time after the said 24th day of June, 1736, be made in any other manner or form than by this Act directed and appointed, shall be absolutely and to all intents and purposes null and void."

Section 2 before set forth was explained by the Act of 9 George IV., cap. 85, to prevent purchases and subsequent conveyances for valuable consideraation from being null and void by reason of the death of the grantor within twelve calendar months after the sealing and delivering of the deed, and not entirely to exempt such conveyances from the Act. It is therefore advisable in the case of a purchase for valuable consideration by a charity to comply with the conditions of section 1. The statute last quoted confirmed all purchases and conveyances for valuable consideration made prior thereto for charitable uses taking immediate effect in possession, which had not been already annulled, or were the subject of legal contention at the passing of the Act.

"Charitable use" has been held to comprise every public, religious, philanthropic, or benevolent object; but not a private charity, as a gift to such objects of benevolence as the trustee in his discretion should most approve (Morice v. Bishop of Durham, 9 Vesey, 399); or to trustees to be applied by them and the officiating ministers of a Methodist congregation as they should think fit to apply the same (Doe v. Copestake, 6 East, 328); or to the Mayor of Dublin for such objects as he should deem most deserving (Harris v. Du Pasquier, 26 L. T., 689); or to a friendly society (in re Clark, 1 Ch. D., 497).

The statute extends to land of copyhold tenure equally as to freehold hereditaments (Arnold v. Chapman, 1 Vesey Senior, 108; Doe d. Howson v. Waterton, 3 Barn. & Ald., 149). The conveyance to a religious or charitable use must take effect immediately in possession. If the operation of the conveyance be postponed for any period of time long or short, or if there be in it any reservation of a portion of the property in quantity or interest, or any use or trust declared or benefit reserved in favour of the grantor, it is void (Lambrey v. Gurr, 6 Maddox, 151). If land granted to such use be subject to a lease, all the grantor's interest in the rent reserved from the lessee and otherwise must be conveyed with the reversion, or the grant will be void (Wickham v. Marquis of Bath, 11 Jurist N. S., 988).

The Act 26 and 27 Victoria, cap. 106, enacts that every deed or assurance by which any land shall have been demised for any term of years for any charitable use shall for all the purposes of the said Act of 9 George II., cap. 36, and of certain other Acts therein referred to, be deemed to have been made to take effect for the charitable use thereby intended immediately from the making thereof, if the term for which such land shall have been thereby demised was thereby made to commence and take effect in possession at any time within one year from the date of such deed or assurance; and 27 Victoria, cap. 13, section 4, declares that every full and *bonâ fide* valuable consideration within the meaning of the said Acts, which shall consist wholly or partly of a rent or other annual payment reserved or made payable to the vendor or grantor, or to any other person, shall for the purposes of the said 9 George II., cap. 36, be as valid and have the same force and effect as if such consideration had been a sum of money actually paid at or before the making of such conveyance without fraud or collusion.

A declaration or trust that the grantor's tomb shall be repaired by the grantee will not avoid a conveyance of land for a religious use. (Doe d. Thompson v. Pitcher, 3 Maule & Selwyn, 407; Lloyd v. Lloyd, 2 Sim. N. S., 255); but a trust for the perpetual repair of a monument in the church itself is a charitable trust within the Mortmain Act (Hoare v. Osborne, 1 L. R. Eq., 585). The reservation by the grantor of power to appoint the ministers or pastors of a chapel conveyed to trustees for the use of the church and congregation, or to make further directions for its better management, does not render the conveyance void (Grieves v. Case, 2 Cox, 301). A gift of impure personalty to trustees, to be divided among such charities in England as they should think proper, is valid (Lewis v. Allenby, 10 L. R. Eq., 668).

If a conveyance for a religious or charitable use be void for non-compliance with any of the conditions prescribed by the statute, the grantor himself or his heir at law may take advantage of the defect, and recover the property in ejectment, or now by action (Doe d. Wellard v. Hawthorn, 2 Barnewall & Alderson, 96; Doe d. Preece v. Howells, 2 Barnewall & Adolphus, 744; Attorney-General v. Munby, 1 Mer., 327; Fisher v. Brierly, 1 De Gex, F. & J., 643; Doe v. Wright, 2 Barn. & Ald., 710). It is sufficient if the deed of conveyance be executed by the grantor alone previously to enrolment, the previous execution thereof by the grantees being unnecessary (Grieves v. Case, 2 Cox, 301, 4 Brown, C. C., 67); and the retention by the grantor of the deed of conveyance after he executed it is immaterial (Attorney-General v. Munby, 1 Mer., 327). The courts will not presume the enrolment of the deed of conveyance after a considerable time from its execution, but the fact must be proved (Doe d. Howson v. Waterton, supra; Wright v. Smithies, 10 East, 409). It was held by Mr. Justice Patteson, and afterwards confirmed by the full court on motion to reverse his decision, that the statute applied to the original or first deed of conveyance of land or property for a religious use or charitable object, which alone required compliance with the conditions therein prescribed, and that every subsequent disposition or dealing with it was unaffected by the Act, on the ground that being once in mortmain it remained so (Walker v. Richardson, T. T., 1837, Exchequer, 2, Meeson & Welsby, 882). A deed of conveyance from old to new trustees, of property already in mortmain by a compliance with the statute, would not therefore require to be made in conformity with section 1, but would be sufficient if executed as an ordinary deed. Nevertheless, some religious bodies, as the Wesleyan Conference, *ex abundanti cautela*, require their people to have every subsequent disposition and dealing with the chapel property made, executed, and enrolled in conformity with section 1 of the statute, although the precaution is unnecessary, see Ashton v. Jones, 16 Jurist N. S., 970.

To bring the conveyance within the protection of the second section of a *bonâ fide* purchase for full and valuable consideration actually paid at or before the making thereof, it has been decided that the money or consideration must be paid to the grantor by the person or party for whose benefit the conveyance is made. If paid to any other person than the grantor, or by any other person or persons than those who derive its benefit, the conveyance is void unless made in strict compliance with section 1. Thus, where a person in custody for having left his family chargeable to a parish in consideration of the sum of £174 having been expended by the parish officers in maintaining them, conveyed land for sixty years, if he should so long live, to the churchwardens and overseers for the time being of the parish, in trust to apply the current rents and profits in aid of the poor's rate, it was held that the deed of conveyance must have been made in conformity with section 1, because the consideration was not paid by the persons who received the conveyance and its benefits, but out of rates levied upon former ratepayers, the previous parishioners generally (Doe d. Preece v. Howells, supra). Where a person possessed of a piece of land for a term of years, in 1796, built at his own expense a chapel on part of it, and in 1806 a sum of £800 was subscribed by the congregation and applied to enlarge and improve the chapel, whereupon and in consideration thereof the original lessee granted an underlease for twenty-three years by ordinary deed to twelve persons of the chapel for the worship of Almighty God by a society or congregation of Protestants under the patronage of the Trustees of the Countess of Huntingdon's College, at the rent of a peppercorn during the life of the grantor, and afterwards of £10 yearly during the residue of the term, it was held that the transaction did not come within the protection of section 2, because the £800 was not a valuable consideration paid to the lessor for granting the demise, but was money expended for the convenience of the congregation in enlarging and improving their chapel (Doe d. Wellard v. Hawthorn, supra). When the religious or charitable uses are declared by a deed separate from the conveyance of the property, the first mentioned alone requires to be enrolled (24 Victoria, cap. 9, sect. 2).

A gift by will of land, or of any estate, term or interest long or short in it, or of any rent, profit or easement out of land, for a religious or charitable use, is null and void by the statute.

A bequest of leasehold land to a religious or charitable use is void, whether specific (Shanley v. Baker, 4 Vesey, 732; Attorney-General v. Tomkins, Amb. 216; Attorney-General v. Tyndall, 2 Eden,

207, S.C. Amb. 614; Hone v. Medcraft, 1 Brown, C.C., 261), or general by a residuary gift (Attorney-General v. Graves, Amb. 155–158; White v. Evans, 4 Vesey, 21; Pickering v. Lord Stamford, 2 Vesey Junior, 272, 581; Paice v. Archbishop of Canterbury, 14 Vesey, 368; Johnston v. Swann, 3 Maddox, 467).

A gift by will of any money charged upon or payable out of land is void, as the proceeds of the sale of land (Attorney-General v. Weymouth, Amb. 20; Brook v. Badley, L. R. 3, C.A., 672; Cadbury v. Smith, L. R. 9 Eq., 37; Ashworth v. Munn, 14 L. J. Ch., 747); or of money due on mortgage, legal or equitable, of or being a lien on land (Attorney-General v. Meyrick, 2 Vesey Senior, 44; Attorney-General v. Caldwell, Amb. 635; White v. Evans, 4 Vesey, 21; Waterhouse v. Holmes, 2 Sim., 162; Symons v. Marine Society, 2 Giff., 325); or due on the security of turnpike tolls, or of the poor or county rates (Knapp v. Williams, 4 Vesey, 430 n.; Finch v. Squire, 10 Vesey, 41; Ion v. Ashton, 28 Beavan, 379); or a judgment debt registered against the land of the debtor (Colluson v. Pater, 2 Russell & Mylne, 344), is void. The Master of the Rolls has recently decided that moneys secured by the bonds of justices in quarter sessions assembled, and charged on the police rates of a division of the county, are pure personalty and may be bequeathed to a charity (re Harris; Jacson

v. Governors of Queen Anne's Bounty, 43 L. T. Rep. N. S., 116).

A gift by will of the unpaid purchase money due on the sale of land (Harrison v. Harrison, 1 Russell & Mylne, 71; Brook v. Badley; Cadbury v. Smith, supra), or on the sale of the growing crops of land (Symons v. Marine Society, supra), is void.

A bequest of money charged on the rates and tolls raised under an act of parliament for improving the navigation of a river, and which is not thereby declared to be personal estate, has been holden to be void (Ion v. Ashton, supra); as also of a mortgage of the "works, rents, and rates," under a town's general Improvement Act (Chandler v. Howell, 4 Ch. D., 651).

A devise of the future rent of land for a religious or charitable use is void, but a bequest of rent then in arrear has been holden valid (Edwards v. Hall, 11 Hare, 13).

A bequest for such use of interest in arrear of a mortgage of land has been declared void (Alexander v. Brame, 7 Jurist N. S., 889). *A fortiori*, would such a bequest of the accruing interest of a mortgage of land be invalid.

A bequest of money to redeem a mortgage upon real or leasehold property, where the equity of redemption is vested in trustees for a charity, is void. Thus where a testator directed the residue of his estate to be sold, and the money arising therefrom to be invested by his trustees in the public funds, and the dividends therefrom to be paid to his wife for her life, and afterwards to raise and pay £500 part thereof to the trustees of a certain chapel to be applied by them in discharging a mortgage thereon; it appeared that the chapel was conveyed to a mortgagee in fee for securing £1000 and interest, which had been paid off and discharged out of the chapel funds and the chapel was reconveyed to the trustees in the lifetime of the testator and before the date and execution of his will. The court held that the legacy was to be applied in the purchase of an interest in land, or of a charge or incumbrance affecting land, and that it became within the third section of the Mortmain Act and therefore void (Corbyn v. French, 4 Vesey, 418).

A bequest of money or other personalty to pay off a debt secured by an equitable mortgage of or being a lien on land belonging to a charity is void. A testatrix by her will gave all her personal estate to trustees upon trust (*inter alia*) to pay thereout £400 to the trustees or treasurer of a Methodist chapel, to be applied in the first place in discharging any debt which might be owing thereon, and the surplus for such purposes of the said chapel as the trustees or treasurer should think fit. There was at the death of the testatrix a debt of £439

12s. 7d. due to the subscribers, who claimed to be equitable mortgagees and to have a lien on the title deeds which were in their possession for the repayment thereof, but there was no other debt owing. The court held the bequest to be void for the reasons assigned in the last cited case. (Waterhouse v. Holmes, 2 Simons, 162.) But a bequest of money to pay debts incurred in respect of a chapel, not being a charge or lien upon it, is valid (Bunting v. Marriott, 19 Beavan, 163).

A gift by will for a religious or charitable use is void by the statute, if the object be to secure to it the possession or enjoyment of land, as of money, on condition that the legatee will furnish land for such use (Attorney-General v. Davies, 9 Vesey, 535; Attorney-General v. Hull, 9 Hare, 647; Langstaff v. Remuson, 1 Drewry, 28); or a devise of land, provided the devisee pay a sum of money to the executors who are directed to apply the residue of the estate comprising land to a charity, in which case the bequest of the money is void and will enure for the benefit of the testator's heir-at-law (Arnold v. Chapman, 1 Vesey Senior, 108; Poor v. Mial, Mad. and G. 32).

But a gift by will of money due on a policy of assurance, for a religious or charitable use, is good, although the company's assets include real property which is liable to pay the sum assured (Marsh v.

Attorney-General, 5 Beavan, 433). *Generally* shares in joint-stock companies, including gas, canal, dock, and railway companies, though part of their capital consist of land necessarily acquired for the purposes of their undertaking (Morris v. Glyn, 27 Beavan, 218; Myers v. Perigal, 2 De Gex, M. and G., 599; Edwards v. Hall, 11 Hare, 13; Taylor v. Lindley, 2 De Gex, F. and G., 599); or in mining companies (Hayter v. Tucker, 4 K. and J., 243; Entwisle v. Davies, L. R. 4 Equity, 272); whether the act by which the company is incorporated does or does not contain a clause declaring that the shares shall be deemed to be personal estate; are not interests in land within the prohibition of 9 George II., cap. 36, unless the share or interest bequeathed should in the ordinary course of events specifically vest in the holder thereof a portion of such land. A bequest to a charity of $3\frac{1}{2}$ per cent. consolidated stock in the Metropolitan Board of Works has been holden void (Cluff v. Cluff, 2 Ch. D., 222). It is now settled that the debentures of railway and other companies executed in the mortgage form of the undertaking pursuant to the "Companies Clauses Consolidation Act, 1845," Schedule C, may be bequeathed to a religious or charitable use (Holdsworth v. Davenport, 3 Ch. D., 185; Mitchell v. Moberly, 3 Ch. D., 655; Attree v. Hawe, 9 Ch. D., 337).

It has been held that the object of the statute is to prevent the augmentation of the quantity of land already in mortmain, and that a gift by will of money to be applied wholly in erecting, enlarging, or improving a church, chapel, or other building connected therewith, standing or being upon such land, is valid (Harris v. Barnes, Amb. 651; Webley v. Dobson, 4 Russell, 342; Glubb v. Attorney-General, Amb. 373; Attorney-General v. Bishop of Chester, 1 Brown, 444; Foy v. Foy, 1 Cox, 165; Attorney-General v. Munby, 1 Mer., 327). But if the testator direct the erection of a church, chapel, school or other building, to render such a gift valid he must specify the land already in mortmain on which it is to be (Giblett v. Hobson, 5 Simons, 651; 3 M. & K., 517; Attorney-General v. Hyde, 2 Amb., 750; Pritchard v. Arbouin, 3 Russell, C.C., 456; Attorney-General v. Davies, 9 Vesey, 535; Attorney-General v. Nash, 3 Brown, C.C., 526; Attorney-General v. Hodgson, 15 Simons, 146; Cox v. Davie, 7 Ch. D., 204).

A bequest of money for the erection or repair of a church, chapel, or building on land already in mortmain (Attorney-General v. Davies, 9 Vesey, 535; Attorney-General v. Chester, 1 Brown, C.C., 444; Fisher v. Brierley, 1 De Gex, F. and J., 643), or for the endowment of churches or chapels in existence (Edwards v. Hall, 13 De Gex, M. and G.,

599), is not prohibited by the Mortmain Acts. Where a testator directed his charity legacies to be paid out of his pure personalty, the specialty creditors, who would have exhausted the personal estate, were ordered to be paid out of the realty (Attorney-General v. Lord Mountmorris, 1 Dick, 379). The statute 33 and 34 Victoria, cap. 34, empowers trustees of charity funds to invest them on mortgage of land, but the property comprised in it must be sold and not foreclosed to realize the security.

A devise of land or bequest of money for a religious or charitable use, rendered void by the Statute of Mortmain, lapses to the heir at law of the testator (Arnold v. Chapman, 1 Vesey Senior, 108; Gibbs v. Rumsey, 2 Vesey and B., 294), or to his nearest of kin (House v. Chapman, 4 Vesey, 542), or sinks to increase the residuary estate of the testator (Cook v. Stationers' Company, 3 Mylne & Keene, 262; Henchman v. Attorney-General, idem 485).

The Legislature has in its wisdom from time to time passed several acts of parliament mitigating the rigour of the Statute of Mortmain. The Act of 48 George III., cap. 108, provides that all persons may by will executed for three months at least before death bequeath all their estate in real property, not exceeding five acres, or goods and chattels not exceeding £500 value, for erecting, rebuilding, repairing, purchasing, or providing any church or chapel where the Liturgy of the Church of England shall be used, or any mansion house for the residence of any minister of the Church of England officiating in such church or chapel, or any outbuildings, churchyard, or glebe for the same respectively; vide Dixon v. Baker, 3 Young and C., 677: and that any such gift exceeding five acres or £500 shall be reduced by an order of the Lord High Chancellor to those limits, on petition to that purport, and that no glebe containing upwards of fifty acres shall be augmented by more than one acre.

Another important exemption from the operation of 9 George II., cap. 36, is contained in 36 and 37 Victoria, cap. 50 (printed *in extenso* in the Appendix, *post*), which enacts that any person or persons being seised or entitled in fee simple, fee tail, or for life or lives of or to any manor or land of freehold tenure, and having the beneficial interest therein, and being in possession for the time being, may grant convey or enfranchise by way of gift, sale, or exchange in fee simple or for any term of years any quantity not exceeding one acre of such land, not being part of a demesne or pleasure ground attached to any mansion house, as a site for a church, chapel, meeting house, or other place of Divine worship, or for the residence of a minister officiating in such place of worship, or in any place of worship within one mile of such site, or for a burial place, or any number of such sites, provided that each such site does not exceed the extent of one acre, and that all gifts, grants, conveyances, assurances, and leases of any site as aforesaid may be in the form therein set forth, or as near as the circumstances will admit, to the execution of which by each party thereto one witness shall be sufficient; and the assurance if otherwise lawful shall be valid, although the donor or grantor shall die within twelve calendar months from the execution thereof. The same privileges are extended to lands of copyhold tenure, if the provisions of "The Lands Clauses Consolidation Act, 1845," are observed with reference thereto.

It is presumed that the privileges conferred by this Act are confined to a grant of *land* only, and that if there be a church, chapel, or house upon it at the time of the execution of the conveyance, the case would not be within the exemption. It is also pretty clear that a grant of rent, profit, or easement out of land is not within the exemption.

The other acts of parliament mitigating the provisions of the Statute of Mortmain are the following, which are printed *verbatim* in the Appendix, *post*, namely: 4 and 5 Victoria, 1841, cap. 38, entitled "An Act to afford further Facilities for the Conveyance and Endowment of Sites for Schools." 13 and

14 Victoria, 1850, cap. 28, entitled "An Act to render more simple and effectual the Titles by which Congregations or Societies for Purposes of Religious Worship or Education in England and Ireland hold Property for such Purposes." 24 Victoria, 1861, cap. 9, entitled "An Act to amend the Law relating to the Conveyance of Land for Charitable Uses." 25 Victoria, 1862, cap. 17, entitled "An Act to extend the Time for making Enrolments under the Act passed in the last Session of Parliament, 24 Victoria, cap. 9." 27 Victoria, 1864, cap. 13, entitled "An Act to further extend the Time for making Enrolments under the Act 24 Victoria, cap. 9, and otherwise to amend the said Law." 29 and 30 Victoria, 1866, cap. 57, entitled "An Act to make further Provision for the Enrolment of certain Deeds, Assurances and other Instruments relating to Charitable Uses." 31 and 32 Victoria, 1868, cap. 44, entitled "An Act for facilitating the Acquisition and Enjoyment of Sites for Buildings for Religious, Educational, Literary, Scientific, and other Charitable Purposes." 33 and 34 Victoria, 1870, cap. 34, entitled "An Act to amend the Law as to the Investment on Real Securities of Trust Funds held for Public and Charitable Purposes." 34 Victoria, 1871, cap. 13, entitled "An Act to facilitate Gifts of Land for Public Parks, Schools, and Museums." 36 and 37 Victoria, 1873, cap. 50, entitled

"An Act to afford further Facilities for the Conveyance of Land for Sites for Places of Religious Worship and for Burial Places." And 38 and 39 Victoria, 1875, cap. 68, entitled "An Act for making further Provision respecting the Department of Science and Art."

The land for the site of the place of religious worship having been granted or conveyed in conformity with the provisions of the Statute of Mortmain as amended by the said other acts of parliament, and the chapel or meeting house having been erected, the next step was to have had it certified by the minister or pastor to the court of general quarter sessions of the peace for the county riding or division in which it lay, as a building for public religious worship by the body or denomination to which it belonged, pursuant to the Toleration Acts, or since 30th July, 1855, to the Registrar General of Births, Marriages, and Deaths, by the minister or pastor or a trustee or trustees or any other person interested therein, pursuant to 18 and 19 Victoria, cap. 81, to entitle the chapel or meeting house and the society or congregation assembling therein with the minister or pastor to the protection of the Acts 52 George III., cap. 155, and 23 and 24 Victoria, cap. 32; passed for the punishment of persons who wilfully disturb a religious congregation or molest the preacher within a building so certified. Section 12 of 52 George III., cap. 155, enacted that "if any person or persons at any time after the passing of this Act do and shall wilfully and maliciously or contemptuously disquiet or disturb any meeting, assembly, or congregation of persons assembled for religious worship, permitted or authorised by this Act or any former act or acts of parliament, or shall in any way disturb, molest, or insult any preacher, teacher, or person officiating at such meeting, assembly, or congregation, or any person or persons there assembled, such person or persons so offending upon proof thereof before any justice of the peace by two or more credible witnesses, shall find two sureties to be bound by recognizances in the penal sum of fifty pounds to answer for such offence, and in default to remain till the next general or quarter sessions, and upon conviction of the said offence at the said general or quarter sessions shall suffer the pain and penalty of forty pounds." Each defendant to an indictment on this statute is liable on conviction to a penalty of forty pounds (R. v. Hube, 5 Term Reports, 542; see also R. v. Cheere, 4 Barnewall & Cresswell, 902).

To entitle the place of religious worship and its minister or pastor to the protection of section 12 of the last mentioned Act it was necessary to comply with section 2, which enacted "that no congregation or assembly for religious worship of Protestants (at which there shall be present more than twenty persons beside the immediate family and servants of the person in whose house or upon whose premises such meeting shall be held) shall be permitted unless and until the place of such meeting, if the same shall not have been registered under any former act, shall have been certified to the bishop of the diocese or archdeacon, or to the justices at the general or quarter sessions; and all places of meeting so certified to the bishop or archdeacon's court shall be returned by such court once in each year to the quarter sessions, and all places of meeting certified to the quarter sessions shall be returned once in each year to the bishop or archdeacon, and the bishop or registrar or clerk of the peace shall give a certificate thereof to such person as shall demand the same on payment of 2s. 6d."

Section 2 enacts that every person knowingly permitting or suffering any congregation or assembly for religious worship of Protestants (or Roman Catholics since 2 and 3 William IV., cap. 115; or Jews since 9 and 10 Victoria, cap. 59), or any other body or denomination where more than twenty persons besides the inmates of the house shall be present, to meet in any place occupied by him until the same shall be certified and registered as therein mentioned, should on conviction thereof before two or more justices of the peace forfeit and pay not more than £20 nor less than £1 for every time such congregation or assembly should meet.

Section 3 imposed a penalty of not exceeding £30, nor less than £2, recoverable in like manner, on any person teaching or preaching in any congregation or assembly as aforesaid, in any place, without the consent of the occupier thereof.

Section 5 imposed a penalty of not exceeding £10, nor less than 10s., recoverable in the same way, on every person teaching or preaching in any such congregation or assembly who should refuse to attend to take the oaths and make the declarations mentioned in sections 4 and 5, or before taking and making the same.

Section 11 imposed a penalty of not exceeding £20, nor less than £2, recoverable alike on every person teaching or preaching at any such meeting as therein before mentioned, with the door bolted or barred, or otherwise fastened, so as to prevent any person entering therein during the time of any such meeting.

Sections 4 and 5 enacted that all teachers and preachers and persons resorting to any place of worship thus certified should be exempt from all penalties under statutes relative to religious worship, on condition that such teachers and preachers should take the oaths prescribed by 19 George III., cap. 44 (viz. the prescribed oaths of allegiance and supremacy in 1st William and Mary, cap. 1, sections 6 and 7; with the Declaration against Popery in 30 Charles II., cap. 2, sect. 2; and the profession of Christian belief in 1st William and Mary, cap. 18, sect. 13) when thereunto required by a justice of the peace, of which taking of the said oaths the said justice should give a certificate according to the form in section 8, which should be conclusive evidence.

The Act 52 George III., cap. 155, was passed to supplement and expound the provisions of the former Toleration Acts, namely 1st William and Mary, cap. 18, and 19 George III., cap. 44.

The 18 and 19 Victoria, cap. 86, sect. 1, enacts that after the passing of that Act nothing contained in any previous act of parliament should apply to the congregations or assemblies therein mentioned or any of them: namely (1) to any congregation or assembly for religious worship held in any parish or any ecclesiastical district and conducted by the incumbent, or if the incumbent be non-resident by the curate of such parish or district, or by any person authorised by them respectively; (2) to any congregation or assembly for religious worship meeting in a private dwelling house or on the premises belonging thereto; (3) to any congregation or assembly for religious worship meeting occasionally in any building or buildings not usually appropriated to purposes of religious worship; and that no person permitting any such congregation or assembly to meet as therein mentioned in any place occupied by him should be liable to any penalty for so doing.

The last mentioned statute, section 2, enacts that every place of meeting for religious worship of Protestant Dissenters or other Protestants, and of persons professing the Roman Catholic religion or the Jewish religion, or of any other body or denomination of persons required to be certified and registered or recorded and not already certified and registered or recorded in manner required by law, may, if the congregation should desire but not otherwise, after the date of the said Act, 30th July, 1855, be certified in writing to the Registrar General of Births, Deaths, and Marriages in England through the Superintendent Registrar of the district in which such place may be situate, and such certificate shall be in duplicate and upon forms in accordance with the schedule thereto or to the like effect, which are to be furnished by the said Superintendent Registrar without fee on application, who shall forthwith transmit such certificate in duplicate to the Registrar General, who, after having recorded the place of meeting therein mentioned, shall return one of the said certificates to the Superintendent Registrar to be re-delivered to the certifying party, for which the former is entitled to a fee of 2s. 6d.

Section 4 enacts that any place of meeting for religious worship theretofore certified and registered or recorded in manner required by law, and continuing to be used for religious worship, may be certified in writing to the Registrar General through the Superintendent Registrar, and shall be recorded in like manner as is provided by section 2.

Section 6 enacts that whenever any certified place of meeting for religious worship shall have wholly ceased to be used for religious worship, the persons or one of the persons who certified the same, or the trustee or one of the trustees, or the owner or occupier thereof, shall forthwith give notice to the Registrar General through the Superintendent Registrar that such place has ceased to be used for religious worship, in a form to be furnished by him, and shall sign the notice in his presence.

Section 11 provides that the Registrar General shall, on payment to him of the fee of 2s. 6d., furnish to any person upon request a sealed certificate of the record of any place of worship registered under that Act, which shall be received in evidence in any court of the facts therein mentioned.

23 and 24 Victoria, cap. 32, sect. 2, enacts that any person who shall be guilty of riotous, violent, or indecent behaviour in any cathedral church, parish or district church or chapel of the Church of England, or in any place of religious worship duly certified under the 18 and 19 Victoria, cap. 81, whether during the celebration of Divine service or at any other time, or in any churchyard or burial ground, or who shall molest, let, disturb, vex or trouble, or by any other unlawful means disquiet or misuse any preacher duly authorised to preach therein, or any clergyman in holy orders ministering or celebrating any sacrament or any Divine service, rite or office in any cathedral, church, or chapel, or in any churchyard or burial ground, shall be liable on conviction thereof before two justices to a penalty of not exceeding £5, or at the discretion of the Bench to imprisonment for not more than two calendar months.

24 and 25 Victoria, cap. 100, sect. 36, enacts that whosoever shall by threat or force obstruct or prevent, or endeavour to obstruct or prevent, any clergyman or other minister in or from celebrating Divine service or otherwise officiating in any church, chapel, meeting house or other place of Divine worship, or in or from the performance of his duty in the lawful burial of

the dead in any churchyard or other burial place, or shall strike or offer any violence to, or shall upon any civil process or under the pretence of executing any civil process, arrest any clergyman or other minister who is engaged in, or to the knowledge of the offender is about to engage in, any of the rites or duties in that section mentioned, or who to the knowledge of the offender shall be going to perform the same or returning from the performance thereof, shall be guilty of a misdemeanour, and being convicted thereof shall be liable at the discretion of the court (assizes or quarter sessions) to be imprisoned for any term not exceeding two years, with or without hard labour, and in addition to or in lieu thereof fine the offender and require him to enter into recognisance with or without sureties, for keeping the peace and being of good behaviour for not exceeding one year: section 71.

The next step will be to have the place of religious worship registered for solemnizing marriages therein, pursuant to 6 and 7 William IV., cap. 85, entitled "An Act for Marriages in England," which enacts, section 18, that any proprietor or trustee of a separate building certified according to law as a place of religious worship may apply to the Superintendent Registrar of the district in order that such building may be registered for solemnizing marriages therein, and in such case shall deliver to the Superintendent Registrar a certificate signed in duplicate by twenty householders at the least that such building has been used by them during one year at the least as their usual place of public religious worship, and that they are desirous that such place should be registered as aforesaid, each of which certificates shall be countersigned by the proprietor or trustee by whom the same shall be delivered; and the Superintendent Registrar shall send both certificates to the Registrar General, who shall register such building accordingly in a book to be kept for that purpose at the General Register Office; and the Registrar General shall indorse on both certificates the date of the registry, and shall keep one certificate with the other records of the General Register Office, and shall return the other certificate to the Superintendent Registrar, who shall keep the same with the other records of his office; and the Superintendent Registrar shall enter the date of the registry of such building in a book to be furnished to him for that purpose by the Registrar General, and shall give a certificate of such registry under his hand on parchment or vellum to the proprietor or trustee by whom the certificates are countersigned, and shall give public notice of the registry thereof by advertisement in some newspaper circulating within the county and in the *London Gazette*; and for every such entry, certificate and publication, the Superintendent Registrar shall receive at the time of the delivery to him of the certificates the sum of three pounds.

Section 19 enacts that if at any time subsequent to the registry of any building for solemnizing marriages therein it shall be made to appear to the satisfaction of the Registrar General that such building has been disused for the public religious worship of the congregation on whose behalf it was registered as aforesaid, the Registrar General shall cause the registry thereof to be cancelled. Provided that if it shall be proved to the satisfaction of the Registrar General that the same congregation use instead thereof some other such building for the purpose of public religious worship, the Registrar General may substitute and register such new place of worship instead of the disused building, although such new place of worship may not have been used for that purpose during one year then next preceding; and every application for cancelling the registry of any such building, or for such substitution and registry of a substituted building, shall be made to the Registrar General by or through the Superintendent Registrar of the district; and such cancel or substitution when made shall be made known by the

Registrar General to the Superintendent Registrar, who shall enter the fact and the date thereof in the book provided for the registry of such buildings, and shall certify and publish such cancel or substitution and registry in manner hereinbefore provided in the case of the original registry of the disused building; and for every such substitution the Superintendent Registrar shall receive at the time of the delivery of the certificate from the party requiring the substitution the sum of three pounds; and after such cancel or substitution shall have been made by the Registrar General it shall not be lawful to solemnize any marriage in such disused building unless the same shall be again registered in the manner hereinbefore provided.

APPENDIX.

THE SCHOOL SITES ACT, 1841. (4 & 5 VICTORIA, CAP. XXXVIII.)

An Act to afford further Facilities for the Conveyance and Endowment of Sites for Schools.

[21*st June*, 1841.]

2. AND be it enacted, that any Person being seised in fee simple, fee tail, or for life, of and in any Manor or Lands of Freehold, Copyhold, or Customary Tenure, and having the beneficial interest therein, or in Scotland being the Proprietor in fee simple or under entail, and in possession for the time being, may grant, convey, or enfranchise by way of Gift, Sale, or Exchange in fee simple or for a term of years, any quantity not exceeding One Acre of such Land, as a Site for a School for the Education of Poor Persons, or for the Residence of the Schoolmaster or Schoolmistress, or otherwise for the Purposes of the Education of such Poor Persons in Religious and Useful Knowledge : Provided that no such Grant made by any Person seised only for life of and in any such Manor or Lands shall be valid, unless the Person next entitled to the same in remainder in fee simple or fee tail (if legally competent) shall be a party to and join in such Grant. Provided also, that where any portion of Waste or Commonable Land shall be gratuitously conveyed by any Lord or Lady of a Manor for any such Purposes as

aforesaid, the Rights and Interests of all Persons in the said Land shall be barred and divested by such Conveyance: Provided also, that upon the said Land so granted as aforesaid, or any part thereof, ceasing to be used for the Purposes in this Act mentioned, the same shall thereupon immediately revert to and become a portion of the said Estate held in fee simple or otherwise, or of any Manor or Land aforesaid as fully to all intents and purposes as if this Act had not been passed, anything herein contained to the contrary notwithstanding.

13 & 14 VICTORIA, CAP. XXVIII.

An Act to render more simple and effectual the Titles by which Congregations or Societies for Purposes of Religious Worship or Education in England and Ireland hold Property for such Purposes. [15th *July*, 1850.]

WHEREAS it is expedient to render more simple and effectual the Titles by which Congregations or Societies associated together for the Purposes of maintaining Religious Worship or promoting Education in England, Wales, or Ireland may hold the Property required for such Purposes: Be it therefore enacted by the Queen's most Excellent Majesty, by and with the Advice and Consent of the Lords Spiritual and Temporal, and Commons, in this present Parliament assembled, and by the Authority of the same, That wherever Freehold, Leasehold, Copyhold, or

Customary Property in England or Wales has been or hereafter shall be acquired by any Congregation or Society or Body of Persons associated for Religious Purposes or for the Promotion of Education, as a Chapel, Meeting House, or other Place of Religious Worship, or as a Dwelling House for the Minister of such Congregation, with Offices, Garden, and Glebe, or Land in the nature of Glebe, for his Use, or as a Schoolhouse, with Schoolmaster's House, Garden, and Playground, or as a College, Academy, or Seminary, with or without Grounds for Air, Exercise, or Recreation, or as a Hall or Rooms for the Meeting or Transaction of the Business of such Congregation or Society or Body of Persons, and wherever the Conveyance, Assignment, or other Assurance of such Property has been or may be taken to or in favour of a Trustee or Trustees to be from Time to Time appointed, or of any Party or Parties named in such Conveyance, Assignment, or other Assurance, or subject to any Trust for the Congregation or Society or Body of Persons, or of the Individuals composing the same, such Conveyance, Assignment, or other Assurance shall not only vest the Freehold, Leasehold, Copyhold, or Customary Property thereby conveyed or otherwise assured in the Party or Parties named therein, but shall also effectually vest such Freehold, Leasehold, Copyhold, or Customary Property in their Successors in Office for the Time being and the old continuing Trustees, if any, jointly, or if there be no old continuing Trustees, then in such Successors for the Time being wholly, chosen and appointed in the Manner provided or referred to in or by such Conveyance, Assignment, or other Assurance, or in any separate Deed or Instrument declaring the Trust thereof, or if no Mode of Appointment be therein set forth, prescribed, or referred to, or if the Power of Appointment be lapsed, then in such Manner as shall be agreed upon by such Congregation or Society or Body of Persons, upon such and the like Trusts, and with, under, and subject to the same Powers and Provisions, as are contained or referred to in such Conveyance, Assignment, or other Assurance, or in any such separate Deed or Instrument, or upon which such Property is held, and that without any Transfer, Assignment, Conveyance, or other Assurance whatsoever, anything in such Conveyance, Assignment, or other Assurance, or in any such separate Deed or Instrument, contained to the contrary notwithstanding: Provided always, that in case of any Appointment of a new Trustee or Trustees of or the Conveyance of the legal Estate in any such Property being made as heretofore was by Law required, the same shall be as valid and effectual to all Intents and Purposes as if this Act had not been passed.

II. And be it enacted, That where such Property shall be of Copyhold or Customary Tenure, and liable to the Payment of any Fine, with or without a Heriot, on the Death or Alienation of the Tenant or Tenants thereof, it shall be lawful for the Lord or Lady of the Manor of which such Property shall be holden, on the next Appointment of a new Trustee or Trustees thereof, and at the Expiration of every Period of Forty Years thereafter, so long as such Property shall belong to or be held in trust for such Congregation or Society or Body of Persons or other Party or Parties to whom such Property may have been or shall be conveyed for their Benefit, to receive and take a Sum corresponding to the Fine and Heriot, if any, which would have been payable by Law upon the Death or Alienation of the Tenant or Tenants thereof; and such Payments shall be in full of all Fines payable to the Lord or Lady of the Manor of which such Property is holden, while the same shall remain the Property or be held in trust for such Congregation or Society or Body of Persons; and the Lord or Lady of such Manor shall have all such Powers for the Recovery of such Sums as such Lord or Lady could have had in the event of the Tenant or Tenants of such Property having died or having alienated the same.

III. And be it enacted, That for the Purpose of preserving Evidence of every such Choice and Appointment of a new Trustee or new Trustees, and of the Person and Persons in whom such Charitable Estates and Property shall so from Time to Time become legally vested, every such Choice and Appointment of a new Trustee or new Trustees shall be made to appear by some Deed under the Hand and Seal of the Chairman for the Time being of the Meeting at which such Choice and Appointment shall be made, and shall be executed in the Presence of such Meeting, and attested by Two or more credible Witnesses, which Deed may be in the Form or to the like Effect of the Schedule to this Act annexed, or as near thereto as Circumstances will allow, and may be given and shall be received as Evidence in all Courts and Proceedings in the same Manner and on the like Proof as Deeds under Seal, and shall be Evidence of the Truth of the several Matters and Things therein contained.

IV. And be it enacted, That the Provisions of this Act shall extend to that Part of the United Kingdom called Ireland.

V. And be it enacted, That this Act may be amended or repealed by any Act to be passed in the present Session of Parliament, except so far as the contrary shall be made to appear.

SCHEDULE to which this Act refers.

MEMORANDUM of the Choice and Appointment of new Trustees of the [*describe the Chapel, School, or other Buildings and Property*] situate   in the Parish [*or Township*] of   in the County [*Riding, Division, City, or Place*] of   at a Meeting duly convened and held for that Purpose [*in the Vestry of the said Chapel*] on the [*25th*] Day of [*April* 1850], *A. B.*   of   Chairman.

Names and Descriptions of all the Trustees on the Constitution or last Appointment of Trustees made the   Day of   .

Adam Bell of
Charles Dixon of
Edward Foster of
George Hurst of
John Jackson of
Kenneth Lucas of
Matthew Norman of
Octavius Parker of

Names and descriptions of all the Trustees in whom the said [*Chapel*] and Premises now becomes legally vested.

First.—Old continuing Trustees :—

John Jackson, now of
Matthew Norman, now of
Octavius Parker, now of

Second.—New Trustees now chosen and appointed :—

Benjamin **Adams** *of*
Charles **Bell** *of*
Jonathan **Edmonds** *of*
Richard **Baxter** *of*
John **Home** *of*

Dated this   Day of

William Hicks,   (L.S.)
Chairman of the said Meeting.

Signed, sealed, and delivered by the said *William Hicks,* as Chairman of the said Meeting, at and in the Presence of the said Meeting, on the Day and Year aforesaid, in the Presence of

C. D.
E. F.

[*The Blanks and Parts in Italics to be filled up as the Case may be.*]

---

24 VICTORIA, CAP. 9.

An Act to amend the Law relating to the Conveyance of Land for Charitable Uses.

[17*th May,* 1861.]

WHEREAS by an Act passed in the Ninth Year of the Reign of His late Majesty King George the Second, and intituled

"An Act to restrain the Disposition of Lands whereby the same become inalienable," it was amongst other things enacted, that no Lands or other Hereditaments should be given, granted, or anyways conveyed, settled, or charged for Charitable Uses, unless such Gift, Conveyance, or Settlement should be made by Deed indented and enrolled, sealed and delivered in the presence of two or more credible Witnesses, Twelve Calendar Months at least before the death of such Donor or Grantor, and should be enrolled in the High Court of Chancery within Six Calendar Months next after the Execution thereof, and unless the same should be made to take effect in possession for the Charitable Use intended immediately from the making thereof, and should be without any Power of Revocation, Reservation, Trust, Condition, Limitation, Clause, or Agreement whatsoever for the benefit of the Donor or Grantor, or of any Person claiming under him: And whereas by another Act passed in the Ninth Year of the Reign of His late Majesty King George the Fourth, and intituled "An Act for remedying a Defect in the Titles of Lands purchased for Charitable Purposes," it was enacted that where any Lands, Tenements, or Hereditaments had been purchased for a full and valuable consideration for Charitable Uses, and such consideration had been actually paid, every Deed or other Assurance then already made for the purpose of conveying or assuring the same should (subject as in the now reciting Act mentioned) be as good and valid in all respects as if the several Formalities by the said first recited Act prescribed had been duly observed and performed: And whereas doubts have been entertained with reference to the Assurance for Charitable Uses of Hereditaments of Copyhold or Customary Tenure: And whereas it is expedient to make provision for further remedying Defects and obviating Doubts and Difficulties and as to Enrolment in regard to Deeds and Assurances of Hereditaments conveyed for Charitable Uses in manner hereinafter provided: Be it therefore enacted by the Queen's most Excellent Majesty, by and with the Advice and Consent of the Lords Spiritual and Temporal, and Commons, in this present Parliament assembled, and by the authority of the same, as follows:—

1. No Deed or Assurance hereafter to be made for any Charitable Uses whatsoever, of any Hereditaments of any Tenure whatsoever, or of any Estate or Interest therein, shall be deemed to be null and void within the meaning of the first recited Act by reason of such Deed or Assurance not being indented, or not purporting to be indented, nor by reason of such Deed or Assurance or any Deed forming part of the same transaction containing any Grant or Reservation of any Peppercorn or other nominal Rent, or of any Mines, or Minerals, or Easements, or any Covenants or Provisions as to the erection, repair, position, or description of Buildings, the formation or repair of Streets or Roads, Drainage or Nuisances, or any Covenants or Provisions of the like nature for the use and enjoyment as well of the Hereditaments comprised in such Deed or Assurance as of any other adjacent or neighbouring Hereditaments, or any right of entry on nonpayment of any such Rent, or on breach of any such Covenant or Provision or any stipulations of the like nature for the benefit of the Donor or Grantor, or of any person or persons claiming under him, nor (in the case of any such Assurance of Hereditaments of Copyhold or Customary Tenure, or of any Estate or Interest therein) by reason of the same not being made by Deed, nor in the case of such Assurances made *bonâ fide* on a sale for a full and valuable consideration, by reason

of such consideration consisting wholly or partly of a Rent, Rentcharge, or other annual Payment reserved or made payable to the Vendor or to any other person with or without a right of re-entry for non-payment thereof. Provided always that in all reservations authorised by this Act the Donor, Grantor, or Vendor shall reserve the same Benefits for his Representatives as for himself.

2. In all cases where the Charitable Uses of any Deed or Assurance hereafter to be made for Conveyance of any Hereditaments for any Charitable Uses shall be declared by any separate or other Deed or Instrument, it shall not be necessary, for the purposes of the first recited Act or of this Act, to enrol such Deed or Assurance for Conveyance, but every such Deed or Assurance for Conveyance shall nevertheless be absolutely null and void unless such separate or other Deed or Instrument shall within Six Calendar Months next after the making or perfecting of such Deed or Assurance for Conveyance be enrolled in Her Majesty's High Court of Chancery; and such Enrolment as last aforesaid shall be deemed and treated for all purposes of the first recited Act, and of this Act, as if such Deed or Assurance for Conveyance had declared such Charitable Uses, and had been so enrolled as last aforesaid.

3. No Deed or Assurance heretofore made, and under which possession is now held for any Charitable Uses whatsoever, of any Hereditaments of any Tenure whatsoever, or of any Estate or Interest therein, made really and *bonâ fide* for a full and valuable consideration actually paid at or before the making or perfecting such Deed or Assurance, or reserved by way of Rent, Rentcharge, or other annual Payment or partly paid at or before the making or perfecting such Deed or Assurance and partly reserved as aforesaid, without fraud or collusion, shall for any reason

whatever be deemed to be null and void within the meaning of the first recited Act, if such Deed or Assurance was made to take effect in possession for the Charitable Uses intended, immediately from the making thereof and without any power of revocation, and has been at any time prior to the passing of this Act, or shall be within Twelve Calendar Months next after the passing of this Act, enrolled in Her Majesty's High Court of Chancery.

4. In all cases where the Charitable Uses of any Deed or Assurance heretofore made for Conveyance of any Hereditaments for any Charitable Uses upon such full and valuable consideration as aforesaid, and under which possession is now held for such Uses, have been declared by any separate or other Deed or Instrument, and such Deed or Assurance for Conveyance has not been enrolled in Her Majesty's High Court of Chancery prior to the passing of this Act, but such separate or other Deed or Instrument has been so enrolled, such enrolment shall be deemed and treated for all purposes of the first recited Act and of this Act as if such Deed or Assurance for Conveyance had declared such Charitable Uses, and had been so enrolled as last aforesaid; but if neither of such Deeds nor such Instrument has been so enrolled then it shall not be necessary for the purposes of the first recited Act or of this Act to enrol such Deed or Assurance for Conveyance; but every such Deed or Assurance for Conveyance shall nevertheless be absolutely and to all intents and purposes null and void unless such separate or other Deed or Instrument shall within Twelve Calendar Months next after the passing of this Act be so enrolled; and such enrolment as last aforesaid shall be deemed and treated for all purposes of the first recited Act and of this Act as if such Deed or Assurance for Conveyance had declared such

Charitable Uses, and had been so enrolled as last aforesaid.

5. Nothing in this Act contained shall extend to render null and void or in any manner to affect or apply to any Deed already good and valid by virtue of the secondly recited Act or of any other Act, or to give effect to any Deed or Assurance heretofore made so far as such Deed or Assurance has already been avoided by any suit at Law or in Equity, or by any other legal or equitable means whatsoever, or to affect or prejudice any suit at Law or in Equity actually commenced for avoiding any such Deed or Assurance, or for defeating the Charitable Uses in trust or for the benefit of which such Deed or Assurance has been made; and no Deed, Assurance or Instrument thirty years old, nor any Deed, Assurance or Instrument heretofore executed as to which it shall be proved to the satisfaction of the Clerk of Enrolments in Chancery that the acknowledgment thereof by the Grantor of the Lands or Hereditaments to which the same relates cannot be obtained within Twelve Calendar Months after the passing of this Act, shall for the purposes of the first recited Act or of this Act require acknowledgment prior to enrolment.

6. Nothing in this Act contained shall extend or be construed to extend to the Disposition, Grant, or Settlement of any Property or Estate lying or being in Scotland or in Ireland, nor to make void any dispositions made or to be made to or in trust for either of the two Universities or any of the Colleges or Houses of Learning within either of such Universities, in the first recited Act mentioned, or to or in trust for the Colleges of Eton, Winchester, or Westminster, or any or either of them, for the better support or maintenance of Scholars only upon the foundation of the said Colleges of Eton, Winchester, and Westminster.

25 VICTORIA, CAP. XVII.

An Act to extend the Time for making Enrolments under the Act passed in the last Session of Parliament, intituled " An Act to amend the Law relating to the Conveyance of Land for Charitable Uses, and to explain and amend the said Act."

[16*th May*, 1862.]

WHEREAS by an Act passed in the last Session of Parliament, intituled " An Act to amend the Law relating to the Conveyance of Land for Charitable Uses," time was given for enrolling certain Deeds, Assurances and Instruments therein referred to until the expiration of Twelve Calendar Months next after the passing of the said Act: And whereas the said Act received the Royal Assent on the Seventeenth Day of May One thousand eight hundred and sixty-one, so that the time thereby given for making such Enrolments will expire at the end of Twelve Calendar Months from that day: And whereas from the great number of Deeds, Assurances and Instruments to be enrolled under the provisions aforesaid it is reasonable to allow an extension of time for that purpose: Be it therefore enacted by the Queen's most Excellent Majesty, by and with the advice and consent of the Lords Spiritual and Temporal, and Commons, in this present Parliament assembled, and by the authority of the same, as follows:—

1. The Enrolment of every Deed, Assurance and Instrument which shall be enrolled before the Seventeenth Day

of May One thousand eight hundred and sixty-four shall for the purposes of the said Act have the same force and effect which it would have had if such Enrolment had been within Twelve Calendar Months next after the passing of the said Act.

2. And whereas by the said Act it is enacted that certain Assurances to be thereafter made *bonâ fide* on a Sale for a full and valuable consideration should not be deemed null and void by reason of the consideration consisting wholly or partly of a Rent, Rentcharge or other annual Payment reserved as therein mentioned, and doubts have arisen whether the said Enactment refers to any Hereditaments not of Copyhold or Customary Tenure: Be it therefore declared and enacted, That the said Enactment comprises and extends to all Hereditaments whether of Freehold or of Customary or Copyhold Tenure, and to every estate and interest therein.

3. No Deed, Assurance or Instrument executed previously to the passing of the said Act shall for the purposes thereof require acknowledgment prior to Enrolment.

4. And whereas it is by the fourth section of the said Act enacted that where the Charitable Uses of any such Deed or Assurance for Conveyance as is therein mentioned had been declared by any separate Deed or Instrument, then, if neither of the said Deeds or Instruments had been enrolled it should not be necessary to enrol such Deed or Assurance for Conveyance, but every such Deed or Assurance for Conveyance should be void, unless such other separate Deed or Instrument should be enrolled within such time as therein mentioned: And whereas it may happen that such Deed or Assurance of Conveyance may have been executed before the passing of the said Act, but the separate Deed or Instrument declaring the Charitable Uses

may not have been executed until after **the passing of the said** Act: Be it therefore enacted that the said Act and this Act shall be taken to apply as well **to cases where such** separate Deed or **Instrument shall be or shall have been** executed after as to cases where **it may have been executed** before **the passing of** the said Act, provided **only that, if** not **already executed, it be executed within six months** next after the passing of this Act.

5. In all cases in which **money shall have been really** and *bonâ fide* expended before the passing of this Act, in **the substantial** and permanent Improvement by Building or otherwise, for any Charitable **Use**, of Land of any Tenure whatsoever, of which possession **is now held by** virtue of any Deed or Assurance **conveying or** purporting to convey **the** same, **or** declaring any Trusts or Trust thereof **for** such Charitable Use, all money so expended shall be deemed for the purposes of the said Act equivalent to money actually paid by **way** of consideration **for the** purchase of **the** said Land.

6. Nothing in this Act contained shall extend to render null and void any Deed or Assurance already good and valid.

27 VICTORIA, CAP. XIII.

An Act to further extend the Time for making Enrolments under the Act passed in the Twenty-fourth Year of the Reign of Her present Majesty, intituled "An Act to amend the Law relating to the Conveyance of Lands for Charitable Uses, and otherwise to amend the said Law."

[13*th May*, 1864.]

WHEREAS by an Act passed in the Twenty-fourth Year of the Reign of Her present Majesty, chapter nine, time was given for enrolling certain Deeds, Assurances and Instruments therein referred to, until the expiration of Twelve Calendar Months next after the passing of the said Act, and by another Act passed in the Twenty-fifth Year of Her present Majesty, chapter seventeen, the time for enrolling such Deeds, Assurances and Instruments was extended to the Sixteenth Day of May One thousand eight hundred and sixty-four; and by the fourth section of the said second Act it was enacted that the said first Act and the said second Act should be taken to apply as well to cases where certain separate Deeds or Instruments therein mentioned should be or should have been executed after, as to cases where they might have been executed before, the passing of the said first Act: Provided only, that if not then already executed such Deed or Instrument should be executed within Six Months next after the passing of the said second Act: And whereas it is expedient further to extend the time for making such Enrolment, and otherwise to amend the provisions of the said first and second Acts and the Acts therein recited or referred to: Be it therefore enacted by the Queen's most Excellent Majesty, by and with the advice and consent of the Lords Spiritual and Temporal, and Commons, in this present Parliament assembled, and by the authority of the same, as follows:—

1. The Enrolment of every Deed, Assurance and Instrument which shall be enrolled before the Seventeenth Day

of May, One thousand eight hundred and sixty-six, shall, for the purposes of the said recited Acts, or either of them, have the same force and effect which it would have had if such Enrolment had taken place within the said time by the said Acts respectively limited.

2. This Act shall be taken to apply as well to cases where such separate Deed or Instrument as is mentioned in the fourth section of the said second Act shall be or shall have been executed after, as to cases where it may have been executed before, the passing of the said first Act: Provided only, that if not already executed, it be executed within Six Calendar Months next after the passing of this Act.

3. And whereas it may be impossible in some cases to enrol the original Deed creating a Charitable Trust by reason of the same having been lost or destroyed by time or accident, but nevertheless the Trusts of such Charity may sufficiently appear by some subsequent Deed appointing new Trustees, or otherwise reciting the Trusts created by the original Deed: Be it enacted that in every such case it shall be lawful for any Trustee or other person interested in such Charitable Trust to apply by Summons in a summary way to the Court of Chancery for an Order authorising the Enrolment of such subsequent Deed: And if the Court shall be satisfied, by affidavit or otherwise, that such original Deed has been lost or destroyed by time or accident but that the Trusts thereof sufficiently appear by such subsequent Deed, then it shall be lawful for the said Court to make an Order authorising the Enrolment of such subsequent Deed; and the Enrolment thereof shall have the same force and effect as the Enrolment of the original Deed would have had if the same had not been lost or destroyed as aforesaid.

4. Every full and *bonâ fide* valuable consideration within the meaning of the first section of the said first Act which shall consist either wholly or partly of a Rent or other annual Payment reserved or made payable to the Vendor or Grantor, or to any other person, shall for the purposes of the Statute passed in the Ninth Year of the Reign of His late Majesty King George the Second, chapter thirty-six, be as valid and have the same force and effect as if such consideration had been a sum of money actually paid at or before the making of such Conveyance without fraud or collusion.

---

29 & 30 VICTORIA, CAP. LVII.

An Act to make further Provision for the Enrolment of certain Deeds, Assurances, and other Instruments relating to Charitable Trusts.

[30*th July*, 1866.]

WHEREAS an Act was passed in the Ninth Year of the reign of His late Majesty King George the Second, chapter thirty-six, intituled "An Act to restrain the Disposition of Lands whereby the same become inalienable:" And whereas by a second Act passed in the twenty-fourth year of the reign of Her present Majesty, chapter nine, certain Deeds, Assurances and Instruments theretofore made were, notwithstanding the first mentioned Act, made valid where the same, or any separate Deed or Instrument declaring the Charitable Uses thereof, had been or should be within the time therein mentioned enrolled in Her

Majesty's High Court of Chancery; and by two subsequent Acts respectively passed in the twenty-fifth year of Her present Majesty, chapter seventeen, and the twenty-seventh year of Her present Majesty, chapter thirteen, the second mentioned Act was explained and amended and the time for making Enrolments thereunder was extended and has since expired; and it is expedient that further Provision should be made with respect to certain Deeds, Assurances and Instruments now rendered void for want of compliance with the Provisions of the first mentioned Act: Be it therefore enacted by the Queen's most Excellent Majesty, by and with the advice and consent of the Lords Spiritual and Temporal, and Commons, in this present Parliament assembled, and by the authority of the same, as follows:—

1. Any Trustee, Governor, Director, or Manager of any Charity, or any other person entitled to act in the management of or otherwise interested in any Charitable Trust, may, by Summons in a summary way, and without Service thereof upon any person, apply to the Court of Chancery for an Order authorising the Enrolment in the Court of any Deed, Assurance or other Instrument whereby any Hereditaments of any Tenure or any Estate or Interest therein have or has been or shall be given, granted, or in any way conveyed, settled, or charged for Charitable Uses, or of any other Deed, Assurance or Instrument relative to or connected with any Charitable Trust, and which Deed, Assurance or Instrument ought to have been enrolled, but has not been enrolled within the time by law limited for that purpose, or (where such Deed, Assurance, or Instrument has been lost or destroyed by time or accident, and the Trusts thereof sufficiently appear by some subsequent Deed appointing new Trustees or

otherwise reciting the Trusts created by the original Deed, Assurance or Instrument) for an Order authorising the Enrolment of such subsequent Deed.

2. If the Court shall be satisfied by affidavit or otherwise that the Deed, Assurance or other Instrument conveying or charging the Hereditaments Estate or Interest for Charitable Uses was made really and *bonâ fide* for full and valuable consideration, actually paid at or before the making or perfecting thereof, or reserved by way of Rent-charge or other annual Payment, or partly paid at or before the making or perfecting of such Deed, Assurance, or other Instrument, and partly reserved as aforesaid without fraud or collusion, and that at the time of the application to the Court possession or enjoyment is held under such Deed, Assurance or other Instrument, and that the omission to enrol the same in proper time has arisen from mere ignorance or inadvertence, or from the destruction thereof by time or accident, it shall be lawful for the Court to make an Order authorising the Enrolment in the Court of the Deed, Assurance or Instrument to which the application relates, or of a such subsequent Deed as the case may be, and the same shall thereupon be enrolled accordingly at any time within Six Calendar Months from the date of the Order, and no acknowledgment shall be necessary prior to Enrolment.

3. Every Enrolment made pursuant to an Order of the Court under this Act shall, notwithstanding anything in the first mentioned Act contained, have the same force and effect which by the second mentioned Act, as explained and amended by the two subsequent Acts before mentioned, is given to the Enrolment of a Deed, Assurance or other Instrument, or of a subsequent Deed, by the three last mentioned Acts respectively authorised to be enrolled,

and duly enrolled according to the provisions thereof, and within the time thereby respectively limited.

4. Provided always that nothing herein contained shall affect or apply to any Deed, Instrument, or Assurance, as to which at the time of any such application to the Court of Chancery any Action, Suit, or Proceeding shall be pending for setting aside the same, or for asserting any right founded on the invalidity thereof, or any Decree or Judgment shall have been then already obtained founded on such invalidity.

---

31 & 32 VICTORIA, CAP. XLIV.

An Act for facilitating the Acquisition and Enjoyment of Sites for Buildings for Religious, Educational, Literary, Scientific, and other Charitable Purposes. [13*th July*, 1868.]

WHEREAS it is expedient to afford greater facilities for the Acquisition and Enjoyment by Societies or Bodies of persons associated together for Religious, Educational, Literary, Scientific, or other like Charitable Purposes, of Buildings and pieces of Land as Sites for Buildings for such Purposes: Be it therefore enacted by the Queen's most Excellent Majesty, by and with the advice and consent of the Lords Spiritual and Temporal, and Commons, in this present Parliament assembled, and by the authority of the same, as follows:—

1. All Alienations, Grants, Conveyances, Leases, Assurances, Surrenders, or other Dispositions, except by Will,

bonâ fide made after the passing of this Act, to a Trustee or Trustees, on behalf of any Society or Body of Persons associated together for Religious Purposes, or for the promotion of Education, Arts, Literature, Science, or other like Purposes, of Land for the erection thereon of a Building for such Purposes or any of them, or whereon a Building used or intended to be used for such Purposes or any of them shall have been erected, shall be exempt from the Provisions of an Act passed in the ninth year of the Reign of King George the Second and intituled "An Act to restrain the Disposition of Lands whereby the same become inalienable," and also from the Provisions of the second section of an Act passed in the twenty-fourth year of the Reign of Her present Majesty, intituled "An Act to amend the Law relating to the Conveyance of Land for Charitable Uses:" Provided that such Alienation, Grant, Conveyance, Lease, Assurance, Surrender, or other Disposition shall have been really and *bonâ fide* made for a full and valuable consideration actually paid upon or before the making of such Alienation, Grant, Conveyance, Lease, Assurance, Surrender, or other disposition, or reserved by way of Rent, Rentcharge, or other annual Payment, or partly paid and partly reserved as aforesaid, without fraud or collusion, and provided that each such piece of Land shall not exceed two acres in extent or area in each case.

2. Provided always that the Trustee or Trustees of any Deed or Instrument by which any such Alienation, Grant, Conveyance, Lease, Assurance, Surrender, or Disposition shall have been made, or the Trusts thereof declared, may, if he or they shall think fit at any time, cause such Deed or Instrument to be enrolled in Her Majesty's High Court of Chancery.

3. From and after the passing of this Act it shall not be

necessary to acknowledge any **Deed or Instrument** in order that the same may be enrolled in **Her** Majesty's High Court of Chancery.

---

33 & 34 VICTORIA, CAP. XXXIV.

An Act to amend the Law as to the Investment on Real Securities of Trust Funds held for Public and Charitable Purposes.

[*1st August*, 1870.]

WHEREAS it is expedient to amend the Law relating to the Investment on Real Securities of Trust Funds held for Public and Charitable Purposes:

Be it enacted by the Queen's most Excellent Majesty, by and with the advice and consent of the Lords Spiritual and Temporal, and Commons, in this present Parliament assembled, and by the authority of the same, as follows:—

1. It shall be lawful for all Corporations and Trustees in the United Kingdom holding moneys in Trust for any Public or Charitable Purpose to invest such moneys on any Real Security authorised by or consistent with the Trusts on which such moneys are held, without being deemed thereby to have acquired or become possessed of any Land within the meaning of the Laws relating to Mortmain, or of any prohibition or restraint against the holding of Land by such Corporations or Trustees contained in any Charter or Act of Parliament; and no Contract for or Conveyance of any interest in Land, made *bonâ fide* for the purpose only of such Security, shall be deemed void by reason of any non-compliance with the conditions and

solemnities required by an Act passed in the Ninth Year of King George the Second, intituled "An Act to restrain the Disposition of Lands whereby the same become inalienable."

2. Provided always, that in every case in which the equity of Redemption of the Premises comprised in any such Security shall become liable to foreclosure, or otherwise barred or released, the same shall be thenceforth held in Trust to be sold and converted into money, and shall be sold accordingly; and if any Decree shall be made in any suit for the purpose of redeeming or enforcing such Security, such Decree shall direct a Sale (in default of Redemption), and not a foreclosure of such Premises.

3. The words "Real Security" in this Act shall include all Mortgages or Charges, legal or equitable, of or upon Lands or Hereditaments of any tenure, or of or upon any estate or interest therein, or any charge or encumbrance thereon; and the word "Conveyance" shall include all Grants, Releases, Transfers, Assignments, Appointments, Assurances, Orders, Surrenders, and Admissions whatsoever operating to pass or vest any estate or interest, at law or in equity, in the Premises comprised in any Real Security.

34 VICTORIA, CAP. XIII.

An Act to facilitate Gifts of Land for Public Parks, Schools, and Museums. [25th May, 1871.]

WHEREAS it is expedient to facilitate Gifts of Land for the purpose of forming Public Parks, Schools, and Museums:

Be it therefore enacted by the Queen's most Excellent Majesty, by and with the advice and consent of the Lords Spiritual and Temporal, and Commons, in this present Parliament assembled, and by the authority of the same as follows:—

1. This Act may be cited as the "Public Parks, Schools, and Museums Act, 1871."

2. This Act shall not extend to Scotland or Ireland.

3. In the construction of this Act, the words "Public Park" shall include any Park, Garden, or other Land dedicated or to be dedicated to the Recreation of the public; the words "Elementary School" shall mean a School or department of a School at which Elementary Education is the principal part of the Education there given, and shall not include any School or Department of a School at which the ordinary payments in respect of the Instruction from each Scholar exceed Ninepence a week; the word "School-house" shall include the Teacher's Dwelling-house, and the Playground (if any), and the offices and all premises belonging to or required for a School; and the words "Public Museum" shall include any Buildings used or to be used for the preservation of any collection of Paintings or other works of Art, or of any objects of Natural History, or of any Mechanical or Philosophical Inventions, Instruments, Models, or Designs, and dedicated or to be dedicated to the recreation of the public, together with all Libraries, Reading-rooms, Laboratories, and other offices and premises used or to be used in connexion therewith.

4. From and after the passing of this Act all Gifts and Assurances of Land of any Tenure, and whether made by Deed or by Will or Codicil, for the purposes only of a Public Park, a School-house for an Elementary School, or

a Public Museum, and all bequests of Personal Estate to be applied in or towards the purchase of Land for all or any of the same Purposes only, shall be valid notwithstanding the Statute of the ninth George the Second, chapter thirty-six, and other statutes commonly known as the Statutes of Mortmain.

5. Provided, that every Will or Codicil containing any such Gift or Assurance, and every Deed containing any such Gift or Assurance and made otherwise than for full and valuable consideration, shall in order to enable such Gift or Assurance to take effect under this Act, be made Twelve Calendar Months at least before the death of the Testator or Grantor, and shall be enrolled in the books of the Charity Commissioners within Six Calendar Months next after the time when the same Will, Codicil, or Deed shall come into operation.

6. Nothing in this Act shall authorise any Gift by Will or Codicil of more than twenty acres of Land for any one Public Park, or of more than two acres of Land for any one Public Museum, or of more than one acre of Land for any one School-house.

7. Nothing in this Act contained shall invalidate or impose any restriction or condition upon any Gift or Assurance which would have been valid and free from such restriction or condition if this Act had not been passed.

36 & 37 VICTORIA, CAP. L.

An Act to afford further Facilities for the Conveyance of Land for Sites for Places of Religious Worship and for Burial Places.

[21st *July*, 1873.]

WHEREAS it is expedient to afford greater Facilities for granting Sites for Buildings for Religious Worship and for Burial Places in England and Wales:

Be it therefore enacted by the Queen's most Excellent Majesty, by and with the advice and consent of the Lords Spiritual and Temporal, and Commons, in this present Parliament assembled, and by the authority of the same, as follows:—

1. Any person or persons being seised or entitled in fee simple, fee tail, or for life or lives of or to any Manor or Lands of Freehold Tenure, and having the beneficial interest therein, and being in possession for the time being, may grant, convey, or enfranchise by way of Gift, Sale, or Exchange in fee simple, or for any term of years, any quantity not exceeding One Acre of such Land, not being part of a Demesne or Pleasure Ground attached to any Mansion House, as a Site for a Church, Chapel, Meeting House, or other place of Divine Worship, or for the residence of a Minister officiating in such Place of Worship or in any Place of Worship within one mile of such Site, or for a Burial Place, or any number of such Sites, provided that each such Site does not exceed the extent of One Acre: Provided also, that no such Grant, Conveyance, or Enfranchisement made by any person seised or

entitled only for life or lives of or to any such Manor or Lands shall be valid unless the person next entitled to the same for a beneficial interest in remainder in fee simple or fee tail (if legally competent) shall be a party to and join in the same, or if such person be a minor, or married woman, or lunatic, unless the guardian, husband, or committee of such person respectively shall in like manner concur: Provided also, that in case the said Land so granted, conveyed, or enfranchised as aforesaid, or any part thereof, shall at any time be used for any purpose other than as a Site for such Place of Worship or Residence, or Burial Place, or, in the case of a Place of Worship or Residence, shall cease for a year at one time to be used as such Place of Worship or Residence, the same shall thereupon revert to and become a portion of the Lands from which the same was severed, as fully to all intents and purposes as if this Act had not been passed, anything herein contained to the contrary notwithstanding. The provisions hereinbefore contained with respect to any Manor or Lands of Freehold Tenure shall apply to Lands of Copyhold or Customary Tenure, but so nevertheless that the provisions of "The Lands Clauses Consolidation Act, 1845," with respect to Copyhold Lands (being sections 95, 96, 97, and 98 of such Act) shall for the purposes of this Enactment be incorporated with this Act.

2. The Purchase Money or Enfranchisement Money or Money to be received for equality of exchange on any such Sale, Enfranchisement, or Exchange shall, if such Sale, Enfranchisement, or Exchange be made by any person or persons seised or entitled in fee simple or fee tail, be paid to the person or persons making such Sale, Enfranchisement, or Exchange, but if such Sale, Enfranchisement, or Exchange be made by any person or persons seised or

entitled for life or lives only, then such Purchase Money, or Enfranchisement Money, or Money to be received for equality of exchange, shall be paid to the existing Trustees or Trustee (if any) of the Instrument under which such person or persons is or are so seised or entitled, to be held by them upon the Trusts upon which the Land conveyed for such Site was held, or if there be no such existing Trustees or Trustee to two or more Trustees to be nominated in writing by the person or persons making such Sale, Enfranchisement, or Exchange; and the receipt of any person or persons to whom such Money is hereby directed to be paid shall effectually discharge the person or persons paying such Purchase or Enfranchisement Money or Money for equality of exchange therefrom, and from all liability in respect of the application thereof; and the Trustees so to be nominated as aforesaid shall invest such Purchase or Enfranchisement Money or Money to be received for equality of exchange in the purchase of other Lands or Hereditaments to be settled to the same uses and trusts as the Land conveyed for such Site should have stood limited to; and until such investment, such Purchase or Enfranchisement Money or Money to be received for equality of exchange shall be invested upon such securities or investments as would for the time being be authorised by statute or by the Court of Chancery, and for the purposes of devolution and enjoyment shall be treated as Land subject to the same Uses and Trusts as the Land conveyed for such Site should have stood limited to.

3. Where any person or persons is or are equitably entitled to any Manor or Lands, but the Legal Estate therein shall be in some Trustee or Trustees, it shall be sufficient for such person or persons to convey or otherwise assure the same for the purposes of this Act without

the Trustee or Trustees being party or parties to the Conveyance or other Assurance thereof, and where any married woman shall be seised or possessed of or entitled to any Estate or Interest, manorial or otherwise, in Land proposed to be conveyed or otherwise assured for the purposes of this Act, she and her husband may convey, or otherwise assure the same, for such purposes by Deed without any acknowledgment thereof; and where it is deemed expedient to purchase any Land for the purposes aforesaid belonging to or vested in any infant or lunatic, such Land may be conveyed or otherwise assured by the Guardian of such infant or the Committee of such lunatic respectively, who may receive the Purchase Money for the same, and give valid and sufficient discharges to the party paying such Purchase Money, who shall not be required to see to the application thereof; and in every such case respectively the Legal Estate shall, by such Conveyance or other Assurance, vest in the Trustees of such Place of Worship or Residence; and if any Land taken under this Act be subject to any Rent, and part only of the Land subject to any such Rent be required to be taken for the purposes of this Act, the apportionment of such Rent may be settled by agreement between the Owner of such Rent and the person or persons to whom the Land is conveyed; and if such apportionment be not so settled by agreement, then the same shall be settled by two Justices as provided in "The Lands Clauses Consolidation Act, 1845," section 119: Provided nevertheless, that nothing herein contained shall prejudice or affect the right of any person or persons entitled to any charge or incumbrance on such Land.

4. All Gifts, Grants, Conveyances, Assurances, and Leases of any Site for a Place of Worship, or the Residence of a Minister, under the provisions of this Act, in

respect of any Land, Messuages, or Buildings, may be made according to the form following, or as near thereto as the circumstances of the case will admit: (that is to say,)

'I [or We] under the authority of an Act passed in the
'thirty-sixth and thirty-seventh years of Her Majesty
'Queen Victoria, intituled "An Act to afford further
'"facilities for the conveyance of Land for Sites for Places
'"of Religious Worship and for Burial Places," do hereby
'freely and voluntarily, and without any valuable con-
'sideration, [or, do, in the consideration of the sum of
'   pounds to me or the said
'paid] grant [alienate] and convey [or lease] to *A. B.* all
'[*description of the premises*], and all [my *or* our *or* the
'right, title, and interest of the] to and in the same and
'every part thereof, to hold unto and to the use of the said
'   and his or their heirs, or executors, or
'administrators, or successors, for the purposes of the said
'Act, and to be applied as a Site for a Place of Worship, or
'for a Residence for a Minister or Ministers officiating in
'   , or for a Burial Place, and for no other
'purposes whatever. [*In case the site be conveyed to*
'*Trustees, a clause providing for the removal of the Trustees,*
'*and in cases where the Land is purchased, exchanged, or*
'*demised, usual covenants or obligations for Title may be*
'*added.*]

'In witness whereof, the conveying and other parties
have hereunto set their hands and seals, the   day
'of   .

'Signed, sealed, and delivered by the said   ,
'in the presence of   of   .'

One witness to the execution of the Document by each party shall be sufficient, and any Assurance under this Act shall be and continue valid if otherwise lawful, although the Donor or Grantor shall die within Twelve Calendar Months from the execution thereof.

5. The persons hereinbefore specified may convey, by way of Gift, Sale, or Exchange, any Site or Sites, not exceeding in the case of any one site the quantity aforesaid, for any of the purposes of the Church Building Acts, to the Ecclesiastical Commissioners for England, or as such Commissioners may direct, and such Commissioners may also act as Trustees for the purpose of taking and holding any Sites granted under this Act; and all Conveyances made under this present Enactment shall be deemed to be made under the Church Building Acts, and the Land conveyed shall vest in conformity with such Conveyances and the Church Building Acts.

6. The provisions of this Act shall not extend to Scotland or Ireland.

7. This Act may be cited as "The Places of Worship Sites Act, 1873."

---

38 & 39 VICTORIA, CAP. LXVIII.

An Act for making further Provision respecting the Department of Science and Art.

[11*th August*, 1875.]

BE it enacted by the Queen's most Excellent Majesty, by and with the advice and consent of the Lords Spiritual and Temporal, and Commons, in this present Parliament assembled, and by the authority of the same, as follows:—

1. Any Lands or any Interest therein may be granted or devised to and taken by the Department of Science and Art, for the Purposes of their Charter, or for any Educational or Public Purposes, and may be held by them accordingly subject to the control of Parliament, and may be sold or disposed of by them when the trusts on which they hold the same are consistent with such Sale or Disposition: Provided that the Department of Science and Art, before accepting any such Grant or Devise, shall obtain the consent in writing of the Commissioners of the Treasury or any two of them to their so doing.

2. This Act may be cited as "The Department of Science and Art Act, 1875."

FORMS.

[1.]

DEED OF CONVEYANCE OF A FREEHOLD SITE FOR A WESLEYAN METHODIST CHAPEL (WITH DECLARATION OF TRUSTS BY REFERENCE TO THE MODEL DEED).

THIS INDENTURE made the   day of   in the year of our Lord   between (the Vendor) of the first part, (the Trustees)   of the second part, and (A. B.)   (the Superintendent Preacher for the time being of the Circuit in the Methodist Connexion, in which the piece of ground and hereditaments hereinafter described are situate) of the third part: Whereas the said parties to these presents of the second part, being possessed of certain sums of money, intended to be laid out in the purchase of a piece of ground and hereditaments, and in erecting and building thereon a chapel or place of religious worship, with such appurtenances as may be thought convenient for the use of the People called Methodists, to be settled to the use, upon the trusts, and in manner hereinafter declared and contained or referred to, have, in pursuance of the said intention, contracted and agreed with the said (Vendor)   for the absolute purchase of the piece of ground and hereditaments hereinafter described and conveyed at or for the price or sum of £   Now this Indenture witnesseth that in pursuance of the said agreement, and in consideration of the said sum of £   of lawful English money, by the said persons, parties hereto of the second part, to the said (Vendor)   in hand, paid out of the monies in their hands, as aforesaid, at or before the sealing and delivery of these presents, the receipt whereof he the said (Vendor)   doth hereby acknowledge and doth hereby admit the same sum to be the full and bonâ fide value of and in full for the purchase of the ground and hereditaments hereinafter particularly described; and from the same sum, and every part thereof, doth hereby acquit, release, and discharge the said parties to these presents of the second part and every of them, their, and every of their heirs, executors, and administrators, for ever, He the said (Vendor)   with the approbation of the said (A. B.)   Superintendent for the time being as aforesaid, testified by his being a party to and executing these presents, Doth grant, bargain, sell, alien, release, and convey unto the said parties hereto of the second part and their heirs and assigns All [describe accurately the property to be conveyed]   Together with all and singular houses, outhouses, edifices, buildings, barns, yards, gardens, trees, woods, underwoods, mounds, mines, delfs, quarries, fences, hedges, ditches, sewers, drains, paths, passages, ways, waters, watercourses, lights, liberties, privileges, easements, profits, commodities, emoluments and appurtenances whatsoever to the said piece or parcel of ground, messuage, or tenement, and hereditaments hereby granted or intended so to be, belonging or in anywise appertaining, or with the same or any part thereof respectively, now or at any time heretofore held, used, occupied or enjoyed, or intended so to be, or accepted, reputed, deemed, taken, or known, as part, parcel, or member thereof, or of any part thereof, with their and every of their appurtenances, and the reversion and reversions, remainder and remainders, yearly and other rents, issues, and profits thereof; and all the estate, right, title, interest, inheritance, use, trust, property, profits, possession, claim, and demand whatsoever, both at law and in equity, of him the said (Vendor)   in, to, out of, and upon the same premises, and in, to, and out of, every part and parcel thereof, with their and every of their appurtenances, To have and to hold the said piece or parcel of ground, messuage, or tenement, hereditaments, and all and singular other the premises by these presents granted or otherwise assured, or intended so to be, with their and every of their appurtenances, in possession, immediately from the making hereof and without any power of revocation, reservation, trust, condition, limitation, clause, or agreement whatsoever, for the benefit of the said (Vendor)   or of any person or persons claiming under him Unto and to the use of the said parties hereto of the second part, their heirs and assigns for ever, but nevertheless upon such and the same trusts, and to and for such and the same ends intents and purposes, and with, under, and subject to such and the same powers, provisoes, declarations, and agreements as are expressed, contained, and declared, or referred to, in and by a certain Indenture of Release bearing date on or about the third day of July in the year of our Lord one thousand eight hundred and thirty-two, and made or expressed to be made between John Sutcliffe, Benjamin Garside, Francis Farnell, John Swallow, Thomas Firth, Robert Wilson, Samuel Naylor, John Fearby Sutcliffe, Thomas Fox Sutcliffe, Charles Swallow, John Swallow the younger, Samuel Morley,

Joseph Garside, accountant, William Farnell, and Joseph Garside, wood turner, therein respectively described, of the first part, the Rev. George Marsden therein described of the second part, and James Brown therein also described of the third part, and enrolled in His Majesty's High Court of Chancery on the twenty-fifth day of July one thousand eight hundred and thirty-two; being a Deed made for the settlement, of a piece or parcel of ground and chapel or place of religious worship, with the appurtenances, situate at Skircoat in the Parish of Halifax and County of York, for the use of the People called Methodists, in the Connexion established by the late Rev. John Wesley: And to, for, or upon no other use, trust, intent, or purpose whatsoever; In witness whereof the said Parties to these presents have hereunto set their hands and seals, the day and year first above written.

[2.]

TRUSTS OF A CONGREGATIONAL CHAPEL DEED.

* * * * * *

Upon the trusts, and with and subject to the powers and provisions hereinafter declared and contained; that is to say:—

I. Upon trust at all times to permit the said chapel and premises, and any other buildings that may hereafter be erected on the said ground, to be used, occupied, and enjoyed as a place for the public worship of God, according to the principles and usages of Protestant Dissenters of the Congregational Denomination, commonly called Independents, being Pædobaptists, under the direction of the church for the time being assembling for worship therein and for the instruction of children and adults, and for the promotion of such other religious or philanthropic purposes as the said church shall from time to time direct.

II. And, under the direction of the said church, to permit the said premises to be repaired, altered, enlarged, taken down, and wholly or partially rebuilt, or any other buildings to be erected on the said ground, so as to render the said premises better adapted for the accomplishment of the purposes aforesaid.

III. And upon trust to permit the deacons of, or other persons appointed for that purpose by the said church, to receive all monies and subscriptions given or paid for the use of pews and sittings in the said chapel, or otherwise contributed for the purposes aforesaid; which monies and subscriptions shall, in the first place, be applied in fulfilling the requirements and obligations of the said chapel, and the discharge of all interest on monies borrowed on mortgage of the said premises or otherwise, for any of the purposes of these presents, premiums for insurance against fire, trustees' expenses, and other claims properly payable thereout, and the residue thereof shall be applied for the support of the Pastor, the maintenance of Divine worship in the said premises, and other the purposes of these presents, as the said church shall from time to time direct.

IV. And upon trust to permit such persons only to officiate in the said premises, as stated Pastors, as shall be of the denomination aforesaid, being Pædobaptists; shall hold, teach, preach, and maintain the doctrines set forth in the Schedule hereto; and shall (except as to the present Pastor) have been chosen by the vote of at least two-third parts in number of such of the members for the time being of the said church as shall be personally present at a special church meeting duly convened and held for that purpose.

V. And shall not permit to officiate in the said premises, as a stated Pastor, any person who shall be guilty of immoral conduct, or who shall cease to hold, teach, and preach the doctrines contained in the annexed Schedule, or who shall cease to be of the denomination aforesaid, being Pædobaptist, or who shall have been removed from his office by the vote of at least two-third parts in number of such of the members for the time being of the said church as shall be personally present at a special church meeting duly convened and held for that purpose, and as shall vote on the question.

VI. And upon trust to permit such occasional Ministers or other persons to officiate in the said premises as the stated Pastor, if any, shall appoint, or, if there be no such Pastor, as the deacons or deacon for the time being of the said church shall (unless the said church shall otherwise direct) appoint.

VII. And upon trust to raise such sum or sums of money, when and on such terms as shall be directed by the vote of at least two-third parts in number of such of the members for the time being of the said church as shall be personally present at a special church meeting duly convened and held for that purpose, and as shall vote on the question, by deposit of the title deeds or by mortgage (with or without powers of or trusts for sale) of the said premises, or any part thereof, and to execute all proper assurances for that purpose.

VIII. And when, and in such manner, and on such terms, and subject to such conditions as to title or otherwise as shall be directed by such a vote as last aforesaid, absolutely to sell the said premises, or any part thereof, either together or in parcels, by public auction or private contract, or partly in each mode, or to exchange the said premises, or any part thereof, for any other premises, freehold or leasehold, and in the said respective cases to assure the same accordingly: the premises so taken in exchange to be situate within twenty miles of the premises hereby granted, and to be held upon the same trusts as are hereby declared concerning the premises hereby granted.

IX. And (after making due provision out of any such mortgage monies as aforesaid for all requirements and obligations and the payment of the trustees' costs and expenses) upon trust to lay out the same mortgage monies, or the residue thereof, in or towards the enlargement, rebuilding, improvement, or repair of the said premises, or otherwise for the benefit of the said church (the same nevertheless being for purposes not inconsistent with these presents), as shall be directed by vote as last aforesaid.

X. And (after making provision as last aforesaid out of any such sale monies as aforesaid, and also for the discharge of all incumbrances and claims on or in respect of the said premises, or of the trusts and provisions hereof) upon trust to lay out the same sale monies, or the residue thereof, in or towards the erection or purchase of such other chapel and premises, freehold or leasehold (the same being situate within twenty miles of the premises hereby granted), at such price, with such title, on such terms, and in such manner as shall be directed by vote as last aforesaid, and to be held upon the trusts hereby declared concerning the premises hereby granted; and until the same shall be required for that purpose, such monies shall be invested in the public Funds, and the annual income shall from time to time be applied in like manner as the monies mentioned in Clause III. are by that clause directed to be applied.

XI. And upon trust (after making provision as last aforesaid out of any monies received on any such exchange as aforesaid) to lay out the same monies, or the residue thereof, as hereinbefore mentioned, with reference either to mortgage or sale monies, as shall be directed by vote as last aforesaid.

XII. And upon trust from time to time to demise the said premises, or any part thereof, when, for such period, at such rent, and upon such terms and conditions as shall be directed by vote as last aforesaid. But it is expressly declared that the reversion in the premises so demised shall continue subject to the powers of mortgaging, selling, and exchanging respectively herein contained. And it is further declared that any rent reserved on any such demise shall be applicable in the manner prescribed by Clause III. respecting the monies therein mentioned, and any fine received on any such demise shall be applicable in the manner prescribed by Clause XI. respecting exchange monies.

XIII. And if the said church shall be dissolved or dispersed, and not be again formed within six calendar months next thereafter, or if the stated public worship of God in the said premises shall be discontinued for two years together, then, and in either of the said cases, upon trust, to let, sell, or otherwise dispose of the said premises, or any part thereof, and to deal with the net monies received for or in respect of the same, in such manner and for such religious purposes (not tending to the promulgation of doctrines inconsistent with those set forth in the Schedule hereto) as shall be directed by the committee (or the major part thereof) for the time being of the Association or Union of Congregational Pædobaptist Churches for the county, or the district of the county, in which the premises hereby granted are situate, such direction being signified in writing under the hands of the then Treasurer and Secretary, or Secretaries, of such Association or Union; but if there be not then any such Union or Association, or if its committee or the major part thereof do not, within two calendar months next after written application by the said trustees or trustee for that purpose, make such direction as aforesaid, then as shall be directed by the committee (or the major part thereof) for the time being of the "Congregational Union of England and Wales," such last mentioned direction being signified in writing under the hands of the then Chairman and Secretary, or Secretaries, of the said Union.

XIV. Provided always, that the receipts of the trustees or trustee for the time being of these presents, for any mortgage, sale, exchange, rent, or other monies payable in respect of the said trust premises, shall exonerate the persons taking the same from all liability to see to the application thereof; and that it shall not be incumbent on any mortgagee, purchaser, or tenant of the said premises, or any part thereof, or on any person taking the same in exchange, to inquire into the necessity or propriety of any such mortgage, sale, letting or exchange, or its authorisation by these presents, or into the due election of any new trustees or trustee hereunder; and that a statutory Declaration by the person or by any two or more of the persons purporting or claiming to be the trustee or trustees for the time being of these presents, and by two members for the time being of the said church or (if the said church shall have been dissolved or dispersed or the stated public worship of God in the said premises shall have been discontinued for two years together) then by two former members of the said church, that the person or persons purporting or claiming to mortgage, sell, exchange or let as the trustee or trustees for the time being of these presents, or (as the case may be) the major part of them, are to the best of the Declarants' knowledge and belief such trustee or trustees, or (as the case may be) the major part of them, shall be conclusive evidence of such person or persons being such trustee or trustees or (as the case may be) the major part of them. And it shall not be incumbent on any such mortgagee, purchaser, or tenant as aforesaid, to inquire whether the persons making such declaration, as members for the time being or former members of the said church, were truly so described.

XV. Provided also, that when and so often as by reason of death, retirement, incapacity, ceasing to reside in England or Wales, or ceasing to be a member of a Congregational Pædobaptist Church in England or Wales, there shall be not more than five trustees of these presents (or sooner if the said church shall think fit), the vacancies occasioned thereby as aforesaid shall be supplied by the appointment, by the vote of a majority of such of the members for the time being of the said church as shall be personally present at a special church meeting duly convened and held for that purpose, and as shall vote on the question, of so many additional persons of the Denomination aforesaid, being men-members of the aforesaid church or of some other Congregational Pædobaptist church in England or Wales, as (if it can be so arranged) will make up the number of not less than the original number of trustees; whereupon all necessary assurances shall be executed and acts done for vesting the trust premises in such new trustees jointly with the surviving or continuing trustees or trustee. But it is expressly declared that this present power shall not be impaired, or become incapable of being exercised, by reason of the trustees being at the time of the exercise thereof reduced below the number of **five**.

XVI. Provided also, that the major part of the trustees for the time being of these presents shall and may exercise all the trusts, powers, authorities, and discretions hereby given to or vested in the said trustees for the time being, and give all consents required from such last mentioned trustees, as fully and effectually in all respects as the same might have been exercised or given by the whole of such trustees.

XVII. Provided also, that any of the trustees for the time being of these presents may retire from the trusts hereof (whether or not another person be appointed a trustee in his place), on giving two calendar months' written notice of his intention so to do to the then Pastor and deacon, or one of the deacons of the said church (if there shall be such Pastor or deacon), and to each of his co-trustees, or to his co-trustee for the time being, if any; whereupon the requisite assurances shall be executed for vesting the said trust premises in the other trustees. Provided that any such notice sent by post to the last known usual place of abode in England or Wales of any trustee shall be sufficient notice to him under this clause.

XVIII. Provided also, that a special or other meeting (as the case may require) of the said church, for any of the purposes of these presents, may be convened at any time by, or by the authority of, the Pastor and deacons for the time being of the said church, or a majority of them; or by, or by the authority of, the deacons alone, or a majority of them, if there shall be no Pastor, or being such he shall not concur with them in convening such meeting; or by, or by the authority of, the Pastor alone, if there shall be no deacons, or being such they shall not concur with him in convening such meeting; or if there shall be no Pastor or deacon, or being such if they or he shall not duly convene such meeting forthwith after written request to them or him so to do from any seven or more of the members for the time being of the said church, or from the trustees or trustee for the time being of these presents, then by, or by the authority of, such seven or more members or (as the case may be) of the said trustees or trustee: That every such special church meeting as aforesaid shall be convened by public notice, specifying the purpose thereof, given in the said chapel, twice on each of the two Lord's days next preceding such meeting, at the usual time for giving notices during Divine service, and such meeting shall not be held earlier than the Wednesday next following the latter of such two Lord's days; and that like public notice of every other church meeting, for any of the purposes aforesaid, shall be given twice on the Lord's day next preceding such meeting, which meeting shall not be held earlier than the Wednesday following such Lord's day: That for the purposes of these presents those only who have been admitted into the full membership of the said church according to its recognised usages shall be deemed members thereof: That no person shall be entitled to vote at any church meeting who shall not have been a member of the said church during at least the six calendar months next preceding such meeting, provided nevertheless that during the six calendar months next following the formation of the said church all the members for the time thereof being in full membership as aforesaid shall be entitled to vote at any church meeting. That no votes shall be given thereat by proxy, but that such votes may be given by ballot or otherwise, as the said church shall from time to time direct: That both male and female members of the said church shall be entitled to vote thereat on all occasions: That (except as hereby otherwise specially provided for) the vote of a majority of such of the members for the time being of the said church as shall be personally present at any meeting of the said church duly convened and held, and as shall vote on the question, shall for the purposes hereof be deemed and taken to be the vote of and shall bind all the members of the said church: and that the chairman of any meeting of the said church, for any of the purposes of these presents, shall have the casting vote in case of equality of votes on any question. Provided nevertheless that the provisions lastly hereinbefore contained for calling and regulating church meetings shall apply only to meetings of the said church for any of the purposes of these presents.

XIX. Provided also, that a memorandum or minute signed by the chairman of any church meeting for any of the purposes aforesaid, of any resolutions adopted thereat, shall, for all purposes of mortgage, sale, exchange, or otherwise, be deemed conclusive evidence of the adoption thereof at a duly convened and duly held meeting, as by such memorandum or minute shall be expressed; and it shall be presumed that the person subscribing such memorandum or minute as chairman was duly appointed to the office.

XX. Provided also, that in all matters relating to the internal government of the said church the same shall be conducted according to the principles and usages of

Protestant Dissenters of the Congregational Denomination, commonly called Independents, being Pædobaptists; viz. that the members for the time being of the said church shall have full and uncontrolled power to manage and arrange all their internal or church affairs, whether regarding the admission, suspension, or exclusion of members, the election, suspension or dismissal of pastors, deacons, or otherwise howsoever (except only in cases by these presents otherwise specially provided for), according to their own interpretation of the Holy Scriptures.

XXI. Provided also, that every trustee of these presents shall be chargeable only with such monies and effects as he shall actually receive, notwithstanding his joining in any receipt or other act for conformity only, and shall be accountable only for his own acts, receipts and defaults, and not for those of his co-trustees or co-trustee; or for any other persons or person with whom any of the trust monies or effects may be deposited, or for any other loss or damage whatsoever, unless the same shall happen through his own wilful act or default.

XXII. Provided also, that every such trustee shall be entitled to deduct and retain, and also to allow to his co-trustees or co-trustee, out of any monies or effects coming to his hands, by virtue of these presents, all costs, charges, and expenses of and incident to the execution of the trusts hereof.

XXIII. Provided also, that (in addition and without prejudice to the power hereinbefore contained) in case any such trustees or trustee shall be required to pay any money for which they or he shall be liable in relation to the trusts of these presents, and the same shall not be duly provided by the said church or otherwise than by such trustees or trustee, it shall be lawful for them or him, of their or his sole authority, and without the consent, request, or direction of the said church or any member thereof (after the expiration of six calendar months' written notice from the said trustees or trustee, requiring payment of such money, and stating the intention of the said trustees or trustee in case of default to mortgage or sell the said premises as hereinafter mentioned, given to the then Pastor for the time being of the said church if there shall be such Pastor, and to the deacon if there shall be one and only one, or, if there shall be more than one deacon, to at least two deacons for the time being of the said church, or, if there shall be no such deacon or deacons, to at least two members of the committee or other body for the time being, if any, appointed by the said church to act instead of deacons, and also affixed to the doors, or some other conspicuous part of the said trust premises on three successive Lord's days), to mortgage or sell all or any part of the said trust premises when and in such manner in all respects as the said trustees or trustee shall think proper; and out of the proceeds thereof to pay all expenses of and incident to such mortgage or sale, and fully to reimburse and indemnify themselves or himself, the said trustees or trustee so liable, and then to dispose of the net residue thereof (if any) in such manner and for such religious purposes (not tending to the promulgation of doctrines inconsistent with those set forth in the Schedule hereto) as are provided in Clause XIII. And it is hereby declared, that it shall not be incumbent on any mortgagee or purchaser, whose title shall be founded on this clause, to inquire into the necessity for or propriety of any such mortgage or sale as aforesaid, or as to the due appointment of the trustees or trustee acting therein: provided that a statutory Declaration of those facts be made by the person or persons creating or effecting such mortgage or sale.

XXIV. Provided lastly, that in the event of the removal of the said church to another locality the powers hereby vested in the said church in regard to the trust premises shall not thereby be suspended, or in any manner impaired or affected.

The Schedule before Referred to.

1. The Divine Inspiration of the Holy Scriptures of the Old and New Testaments, and their supreme authority as the rule of faith and practice.

2. The unity of the Godhead; and the essential Deity of the Father, of the Son, and of the Holy Spirit.

3. The fall and depravity of man, and the consequent necessity of the grace and power of the Holy Spirit for his regeneration and sanctification.

4. The incarnation of the Son of God in the person of the Lord Jesus Christ; His sacrificial death for the sins of mankind, and the justification by faith of all who believe in Him.

5. The moral freedom and responsibility of man; the unlimited invitations of the gospel; and the election, according to God's gracious purpose, of a multitude that no man can number unto holiness and eternal life.

6. The immutable authority of the moral law of God as the rule of human conduct.

7. The immortality of the soul, the resurrection of the dead, and the final judgment when the wicked shall go away into everlasting punishment, but the righteous unto life eternal.

[3.]

TRUSTS OF A BAPTIST CHAPEL DEED.

* * * * * *

Upon the trusts hereinafter declared concerning the same, (that is to say,) upon trust at all times hereafter to permit the said meeting house and premises to be used as a place of public religious worship by the Society of Protestant Dissenters, called Particular or Calvinistic Baptists, now meeting for Divine worship therein, and also by such other persons as shall hereafter be united to the said Society, and for that purpose to permit to officiate in the said meeting house, and to reside in any house which may be erected upon the same premises for that purpose, such person or persons of the denomination of Protestant Dissenters called Particular or Calvinistic Baptists, as the members of the said Society present at any church meeting duly assembled for that purpose by public notice, to be given in the said meeting house during public worship on the two Sundays immediately preceding such church meeting, or two-third parts of them in number, shall from time to time elect as their Minister or Pastor, during their will and pleasure only. And upon further trust, in case a schoolroom or schoolrooms shall be erected or provided upon the said premises, or if there shall be no separate schoolroom or schoolrooms, and it shall by the members of the said Society present at their church meeting duly assembled as aforesaid, or two-third parts of them in number, be thought necessary or expedient to hold and teach a Sunday or other school or schools in any proper part of the said meeting house, then to permit and suffer a Sunday or other school or schools to be held, conducted, and carried on from time to time in the said schoolroom or schoolrooms, or if it shall be thought necessary or expedient as aforesaid in the said meeting house, but only at such hours and times as shall not interfere with the public worship of Almighty God therein; and in all cases, whether in the said meeting house or not, under such government, orders, and regulations as shall be agreed upon by the members of the said Society present at their church meeting duly assembled as aforesaid, or two-third parts of them in number. And upon further trust to let the pews or seats in the said meeting house upon rent, and to receive all monies arising therefrom and from the voluntary contribution of the church members and hearers assembling therein and otherwise, and to apply the same in payment of the salary of the Minister or Pastor and other purposes of the church. And upon further trust from time to time to raise such sum or sums of money as the members of the said Society present at a church meeting duly assembled as aforesaid, or two-third parts of them in number, shall direct by mortgage or mortgages of all or any part of the said trust estate, and make any conveyance, demise, or other assurance whatsoever for that purpose, including a power of sale and all other usual covenants and powers. And also when thereunto required by the members of the said Society present at a church meeting duly assembled as aforesaid, or two-third parts of them in number, absolutely to make sale of the said hereditaments and premises, either by public auction or private contract, or to exchange the said hereditaments and premises, or any part thereof, for or in lieu of any other hereditaments, whether freehold, copyhold, customary, or leasehold, and make any conveyances or assurances whatsoever for the said purposes, provided always that the trustees for the time being shall stand seised or possessed of the hereditaments and premises which shall be so taken in exchange upon the same trusts as are hereinbefore declared concerning the hereditaments hereby assured, and also shall stand possessed of the money which from time to time shall be received on any mortgage, sale, or exchange, upon trust to lay out and dispose of the same in such manner and for such purposes, for the improvement of the trust property, or the enlargement, repair, or rebuilding of the trust premises, as the members of the said Society present at a meeting to be called for that purpose in manner aforesaid, or two-third parts of them in number, shall from time to time direct. But in case the said Society of Particular or Calvinistic Baptists shall be totally dissolved or dispersed, and the regular public worship at the said meeting house be discontinued by them for the space of twelve calendar months together, then upon further trust to let, sell, convey, and release, or otherwise dispose of the said meeting house, hereditaments and premises, with the appurtenances, to such person or persons, for such term, in such manner, and for such purposes as the managers for the time being of a Society called the Baptist Building Fund, established in London in 1824, or the major part of them, shall from time to time direct or appoint of or concerning the same. PROVIDED ALSO, and it is hereby agreed and declared, that when and so often, during the continuation of the trusts hereby created, as the number of the trustees shall by death, resignation, removal from office or beyond the seas, or incapacity to act, be reduced to five or less, for the purposes aforesaid, or oftener, if the members of the said Society shall think it expedient, so many other persons shall be named and chosen to be trustees, as shall make up the whole number of trustees (nine), such new trustees to be from time to time nominated, appointed, and chosen by the members of the said Society present at their church meeting duly assembled as aforesaid, or two-third parts of them in number, and upon every such choice the continuing trustees for the time being shall by sufficient assurances in the law at the expense of the trust estate or of the funds of the said Society, assure the said meeting house, hereditaments, and premises, with the appurtenances, so and in such manner as that the same may become legally and effectually vested in such new trustees or trustee jointly with any continuing trustees or trustee, or in such new trustees only, as the case may require, upon such or the like trusts, and for such or the like intents and purposes, as are hereinbefore declared, and expressed of and concerning the same premises.

[4.]

TRUSTS OF A CALVINISTIC METHODIST CHAPEL DEED.

* * * * * *

To hold the said premises unto and to the use of the said trustees their heirs and assigns upon trust for the said Calvinistic Methodist Connexion according to the constitution and regulations thereof set forth in the Constitutional Deed declaratory of the objects and regulations of the said Connexion dated the tenth day of August one thousand eight hundred and twenty-six, and accordingly to permit the said chapel and premises to be used as a place of religious worship by a congregation of Protestants belonging to the said Connexion, and to permit such person and persons as shall be approved or appointed according to the regulations of the said Connexion as set forth in the said deed and no other person to preach, minister, and perform other acts of religious worship therein. And also upon trust to let the seats in the said chapel, and to receive and apply the income arising therefrom and all voluntary contributions, and to sell, exchange, mortgage or demise the said premises or any part thereof as the said Connexion or the county monthly meeting of   shire or any quarterly association of the said Connexion in conformity with the provisions of the said deed, and in exercise of the powers thereby conferred, shall direct; and to make and execute all such instruments and do and concur in all such acts as may be needful or expedient for carrying such directions into effect. And it is hereby declared that the said trustees and any trustees or trustee to be appointed as hereinafter provided shall hold the monies to arise from the said seats and contributions, and from any such sale or mortgage, or received by way of equality of exchange and any hereditaments to be taken in exchange upon trust for the said Connexion, and to assure and dispose of the same as the said Connexion or the said county monthly meeting or any quarterly association of the said Connexion in conformity with the said deed shall direct. And also that if any of the said trustees or any trustees or trustee to be appointed as hereinafter provided shall go to reside permanently out of

England or Wales, or shall cease to be a member in full communion with the said Connexion, he or they shall immediately thereupon become absolutely disqualified to act as trustees or trustee, **and upon such** disqualification or upon the death resignation or incapacity of any trustee or at any other time when the said county monthly meeting shall think fit, the said **county monthly meeting acting in conformity with the regulations** of the said deed may appoint any other fit person or persons (being a member or members in full communion with the said Connexion) to be a trustee or trustees in the place of the trustee or trustees so becoming disqualified, dying, resigning, or becoming incapable to act; and upon every such appointment the number of the trustees may be augmented or reduced.

www.ingramcontent.com/pod-product-compliance
Lightning Source LLC
Chambersburg PA
CBHW031740230426
43669CB00007B/416